Praise for *It's Not about the Wine*

"Celeste Yvonne opened my eyes to the toxic Mommy Wine Culture years ago. Admittedly, I didn't understand the harm in it until I read her words. Now I know drinking at night because I 'deserve it' or because 'my kids were a lot' or because 'work was hard' isn't my right; it's the start of a potentially harmful addiction. Celeste Yvonne has changed the narrative and is helping thousands of people change their lives. Her book is a needed resource for women everywhere."

—Leslie Means, founder and owner of
Her View From Home, LLC

"Celeste Yvonne calls out the all-too-common and often dysfunctional relationship our culture has with alcohol. As you read, you will find yourself nodding along, maybe even seeing bits and pieces of yourself in her story. And I guarantee, you will be inspired to get to a healthier place."

—Kate Swenson, author of *Forever Boy: A Mother's
Memoir of Autism and Finding Joy*

"An essential addition to the quit lit genre. Mommy Wine Culture is incredibly insidious, and Celeste Yvonne faces the topic head-on with history, facts, and personal experience. Anyone interested in parenting or motherhood needs to read this book!"

—Amanda White, executive director and licensed
therapist at Therapy for Women Center
and author of *Not Drinking Tonight*

"I'm on the back end of raising my three kids, yet I found myself nodding at every page of this book. Celeste Yvonne addresses the elephant in so many playrooms: the tremendous burden that sits on the shoulders of mothers—and why we often turn to alcohol to cope with parenting challenges. She bravely dissects Mommy Wine Culture and reframes how we should look at supporting mothers, providing practical tips families can implement immediately. This book goes against the grain in the best way possible, and I hope it's the catalyst for more mothers to stop reaching for the bottle and start caring for themselves."
—Whitney Fleming, author, freelance writer, and social media consultant at Whitney Fleming Writes

"*It's Not about the Wine* is a powerful read, from the dedication to the ending. Through stories from Celeste and other strong mothers in recovery, the reader will see how destructive Mommy Wine Culture is. There's one thing for sure: it will help you proudly say no to that drink you don't really want at the playdate and not care what anyone thinks. It's a must-read."
—Danielle Sherman-Lazar, author of *Living Full*

"In *It's Not about the Wine*, Celeste Yvonne deconstructs Mommy Wine Culture as a solution to the mental load of motherhood and flips this ongoing struggle that so many women face completely on its head, paving the path to meaningful motherhood and a beautiful life without the damaging effects of alcohol. Celeste has given us a book that is truly revolutionary, wonderful, and wise—a primer on sober living. Don't miss it!"
—Mikala Albertson, MD, author of *Ordinary on Purpose: Surrendering Perfect and Discovering Beauty amid the Rubble*

"This book has absolutely revolutionized the way I view my relationship with alcohol. True to her title, Celeste masterfully demonstrates just how deeply Mommy Wine Culture has permeated motherhood, drawing insightful connections between her own personal experiences and the ways in which mothers are still unsupported and unequal on a societal level. This is such an important and informative read for *any* mom, regardless of whether she drinks. Thought-provoking, well-researched, and incredibly relevant."

—Emily Solberg, creator and writer behind
Shower Arguments with Emily Solberg

"I wish I had this book during the years I spent riddled with guilt for clinging to unhelpful coping mechanisms, trying to escape the overwhelming weight of motherhood, but I'm glad I have it now. While this book dives deep into the reasons women drink, it does so much more. It is an empathetic and sometimes maddening social commentary on why we feel the need to escape in the first place, the unfair mental load that women and mothers carry, and a helpful instruction manual about how to find solutions that actually help. A must-read for all women!"

—Emily Lynn Paulson, author of *Hey, Hun: Sales, Sisterhood, Supremacy, and the Other Lies behind Multilevel Marketing*, and founder of Sober Mom Squad

"Celeste Yvonne has written such a generous, wise, intelligent account of a pervasive cultural phenomenon and its toxic effects. The book doesn't just dismantle the myths perpetuated about Mommy Wine Culture; it draws a road map for escaping them. And it's clear on every page that *It's Not about the Wine* is a firsthand account by someone who lived it, which is really important. Many readers are waiting for this book, whether they know it or not."

—Jardine Libaire, coauthor of *The Sober Lush*

"The only way to read this book is with your hand on your heart, giving yourself grace and permission to be humbly validated. *It's Not about the Wine* delivers raw emotion with vetted resources, making sense of how we got here and what to do about it. Celeste Yvonne has successfully executed a modern, convincing, and revolutionary way to help us all rethink the role of alcohol in our lives."

—Ashley Reckdenwald, founder and CEO of Working Mom Notes

"You'll see yourself reflected in these pages, not with shame or guilt, but with a keen eye toward all the ways Mommy Wine Culture has manipulated the experience of drinking and motherhood. It's a rallying cry for cultural change and an absolute must-read."

—Gemma Hartley, author of *Fed Up: Emotional Labor, Women, and the Way Forward*

"*It's Not about the Wine* gives us what we need most in the trenches: first, the reassurance that we are not alone, and then the right next steps to help us climb out. Whatever our personal relationship with Mommy Wine Culture, Celeste helps us see that for a lot of us who indulge or even overindulge, the alcohol is a symptom of much bigger societal issues that doesn't get talked about enough, or at least didn't until this book came along."

—Liz Petrone, author of *The Price of Admission: Embracing a Life of Grief and Joy*

"Celeste Yvonne was one of the first sober voices I happened upon when I was first considering removing alcohol from my life. Almost four years later, and she remains one of the most influential voices on sobriety. *It's Not about the Wine* is eye opening and validating. Anyone who has ever, even for a second, had a voice inside themselves whisper 'Why am I drinking?' should give this book a read."

—Alicia Cooke, bestselling poet

It's Not about
the Wine

IT'S NOT ABOUT
THE WINE

The Loaded Truth behind
Mommy Wine Culture

CELESTE YVONNE

Broadleaf Books
Minneapolis

IT'S NOT ABOUT THE WINE
The Loaded Truth behind Mommy Wine Culture

Library of Congress Cataloging-in-Publication Data

Names: Yvonne, Celeste, author.
Title: It's not about the wine : the loaded truth behind mommy wine culture / Celeste Yvonne.
Description: Minneapolis : Broadleaf Books, [2023]
Identifiers: LCCN 2022056264 (print) | LCCN 2022056265 (ebook) | ISBN 9781506486758 (hardback) | ISBN 9781506486758 (ebook)
Subjects: LCSH: Mothers—Alcohol use. | Women alcoholics— Rehabilitation. | Recovering alcoholics—Family relationships. | Women alcoholics—Family relations. | Mothers—Social conditions.
Classification: LCC HV5137 .Y96 2023 (print) | LCC HV5137 (ebook) | DDC 362.292085/2—dc23/eng/20221201
LC record available at https://lccn.loc.gov/2022056264
LC ebook record available at https://lccn.loc.gov/2022056265

Cover design: Olga Grlic

Print ISBN: 978-1-5064-8675-8
eBook ISBN: 978-1-5064-8676-5

To my kids.
I once used parenting as an excuse to drink.
But you are my favorite
reason to abstain.

CONTENTS

CONTENTS

PREFACE

I started writing about motherhood when I was pregnant with Ben, my secondborn. Early in the pregnancy, I had so much anxiety and fear, following a miscarriage earlier that year. But I also felt excited—elated really. This second child would complete our family. I wanted to shout my pregnancy from the rooftops. I had a miracle growing inside me!

Culturally we have an unspoken rule not to announce pregnancy until after the first trimester. God forbid we tell everyone, only to lose the baby later. HoW eMbArRaSsInG. (Is the sarcasm bleeding through the page? I hope so.) What are mothers expected to do when we experience early miscarriage? Wipe the tears, apparently, and move on. Keep our emotions in check, hold our chin up, and keep everyone around us blissfully unaware that a piece of our heart just died.

Our society's ambivalence toward a mother-to-be's preterm loss is perhaps the very first of many messages we send to mothers that their struggles are best remained hidden. No one wants to hear about it, so don't make things weird. And like any dutiful "good mom," I played my part. I stayed in my lane for family and friends. But privately? I had things to say.

I started an anonymous blog I named "And What a Mom" to share this early pregnancy experience, my heartbreak after my miscarriage, and my dreams for my growing family—a virtual diary sent out to the world in the hopes that my words would resonate with a few women who may stumble across my posts.

Over time, my blog's readership slowly grew. I created corresponding Facebook and Instagram pages and those grew as well. The things I wrote about evolved as my family and motherhood experience changed. I stopped posting anonymously and started using a pen name, Celeste Yvonne, to maintain some privacy as I shared my story and delved into the good and bad and all-around messy challenges of motherhood, which I referred to as "The Ultimate Mom Challenge." A post called "Dear Husband" about my grievances with the mental load of motherhood (the invisible work women do to keep a household running) went viral to millions.

The post was written in the form of a letter to my husband, but I hadn't actually left it on his pillowcase one morning after a bleary-eyed night of caring for our newborn. The "letter" was inspired by a conversation my husband and I'd had and was meant as a metaphor for those mothers who, like me, were struggling with the enormity of this new role of mom, even when our existing household duties and other responsibilities remained unchanged.

I wrote about returning to work but feeling undersupported both at home and in the workplace. I wanted to understand why women pushed so hard for equality and liberation, yet when our husbands watched the children, we called it "babysitting." I argued for a more even split of responsibilities and child-rearing on the home front. Mostly, I asked for more help, because if something didn't change, and fast, I would break.

Many women praised my honesty and candor. I received private messages of support, but they also expressed frustration with the mental load of motherhood. They wondered: "*What* brought us here? *Why* aren't more of us speaking up? And *how* do we go forward?"

But not all the feedback was positive. I received hundreds of vile messages from men and women. Some hoped my husband would divorce me; others went so far as to wish me dead. Clearly, I'd touched a nerve. Maybe the world wasn't ready for this conversation yet, and besides, who was I to lead this charge? I retreated. I was too far out of my comfort zone, and I decided to return to writing in the "safe" zone: motherhood, children, and other socially acceptable topics.

The mental load of motherhood sat with me though. I knew there was more to this topic, and I started thinking about where it bled into other aspects of our culture: this expectation to compartmentalize our work and family life, to "bounce back" after pregnancy loss and childbirth, and to make it all look so easy. The BS premise that just being a mother should be all the fulfillment we need.

The burden mothers have been holding for generations had been stuffed down our collective throats, and I could feel it suffocating us all.

Eventually, I did indeed break. The glass of wine I usually drank after the kids went to bed turned into two, three, sometimes the whole bottle. My drinking reached a tipping point where the line between want and need began to overlap. I saw a side of me that wasn't pretty and a behavior that wasn't sustainable. Clearly, numbing myself was not the solution I was seeking.

I reluctantly quit drinking and started to focus on my family. As soon as I stopped leaning on alcohol and started to process my emotions, a feeling came over me that was so strong, I couldn't hold it in anymore. Rage.

I was pissed off. I started thinking about the toxic narrative of our "Mommy Wine Culture"—the pervasive message that alcohol helps mothers survive motherhood—and how destructive this message is. I saw how we conditioned ourselves and each other to believe that our grievances about parenting weren't anything some rosé or a good cabernet couldn't fix.

Mommy Wine Culture was and is a symptom of the larger issue: the mental load of motherhood, a burden born from outdated family norms, traditional roles, and a systematic lack of support for moms.

Drinking was my way of coping with the seemingly insurmountable weight of modern motherhood—a weight that causes countless other mothers to seek solace in pills, weed, and other escapes. But the "mother" of all drugs remains alcohol.

I'll begin the book by asking the two most pressing questions about the mental load of motherhood, Mommy Wine Culture, and the significant rise in female drinking: *what* and *why*. What are we doing to ourselves, and why are we doing it? The rest of the book answers the question *how*. How do we break free from the clutches of alcohol and addiction? How do we find balance, community, and friendship without alcohol? And how do we create a life we don't need to escape from?

Each chapter in the *how* section will start with one or two stories about mothers who are in recovery from alcohol use disorder. Their stories encapsulate the unique challenges of motherhood and the hope in sobriety.

I will also share my own story, including excerpts from blog posts I wrote while I was still actively drinking or in early recovery as I started to question various aspects of motherhood and our drinking culture. Most authors in recovery only tell their stories after years of recovery and reflection. These blog posts give that real, raw sense of frustration, desperation, and a little bit of self-victimization that I think is normal in many people's early days of sobriety. I look back on a few of these pieces and cringe at my tone or relive the sadness and struggle I now know was part of my healing process. This writing reminds me how far I've come, and it offers you a closer glimpse at a mom starting to question her relationship to alcohol, making the decision to quit drinking, and the flood of emotion that comes when someone starts to redefine and take back their life.

Lastly, each chapter will end with tips on *how* to lighten your mental load. The tips are tangible things you can start doing right away, suggestions I wish I'd been offered in my own early sobriety.

When I was chatting with my agent about hopes for this book, she asked me if the goal was to encourage people to quit drinking.

I said no. And even now as I put the finishing touches on these pages, I stand by that answer.

The goal of this book is to look at why we mothers turn to alcohol as a solution in the first place and to help us all find ways to fix the underlying problems we face. While many women may end up making the same choice I did, I'm not writing this book to convince anyone to quit drinking. But I do hope readers learn enough that if you do choose to drink, you do so with informed consent. I hope every time you see a wine meme or an alcohol ad you can look at it with a critical eye and see just who benefits from such a narrative—and at whose expense. I hope every time you meet someone who says "I don't drink" you don't feel shocked or even ask why but instead simply smile and offer them a nonalcoholic alternative (tap water doesn't count).

I hope if you do continue to drink you do so with a healthy awareness of how this substance is affecting your body, your mental health, and your children. And yes, I hope if you choose to try sobriety you can come away from this book understanding that you're choosing an opportunity to live your best life. That abstaining from alcohol is not the end, it's just the beginning.

Once we understand the root of what got us here and why Mommy Wine Culture is selling all of us short, that is where healing and true change begin.

Let me show you how.

PART ONE

WHAT

1 | WHAT IS MOMMY WINE CULTURE?

MOMMY NEEDS MORE WINE

I was a wine mom, often pouring myself a glass of cabernet as soon as the clock struck five, and by bedtime the bottle was empty and I was stuffing it deep into the recycling bin. Some nights were better than others. If I had big plans at work the next day, I'd manage to take it slow. But other nights, my ability to moderate would be MIA. A promise to myself of just one glass spiraled into a full-on binge, and the next day I was left reassembling the pieces of the night through a cloudy head.

I didn't drink every day. When I was alone with the kids, I didn't drink at all. Even when my husband was home, I always waited until after five o'clock to start and I'd be in bed before ten, hoping to sleep off everything by morning.

But still, some mornings after heavy drinking were rough. Really rough. I'd get out of bed because I had to, but it hurt. My head pounded; I was nauseated. I'd have to face the day because I had kids to take care of and a demanding corporate job. But often on weekends, my plans for errands, chores at home, or activities with the kids were thwarted as I nursed my wounds and pushed things off until tomorrow.

From the outside, I looked like a successful, fit, outgoing mom of two little boys. I was a happily married marketing professional who had recently run her first marathon. I was a popular blogger with thousands of followers who wrote about the good and bad of parenting. But secretly, just between me and the four walls of my home, I was a mom with a drinking problem.

My early days as a mom were a huge learning curve. In addition to learning how to breastfeed, how to swaddle, and how to change a diaper without getting peed on, I also started learning how to navigate alcohol in what I thought were the most responsible ways possible.

No one expected me to put the bottle down once I became a parent. Quite the opposite, in fact. The encouragement to drink by friends, family, colleagues, and the media for moms, even new moms, is alarming. I received a few bottles of wine as gifts upon my firstborn's arrival, and friends came over to celebrate with wine and beer less than a week after the baby was born. The assumption that parenthood would lead to regular, if not necessarily increased, consumption was unspoken yet understood. Moms drink wine. Moms self-medicate with booze. Drinking is part of the journey.

And so, I tried to find that "balance" all of us moms are looking for, only for me, that balance was focused around being a mom—even, dare I say it, a "good" mom—and drinking.

In my head, I justified my drinking because (1) I wasn't drinking every day, (2) I was being "responsible," never day drinking and never driving under the influence, and (3) I was functioning at my job and in every other responsibility I had taken on, and I was exercising regularly. I wasn't some worthless drunk, obviously—look at my schedule! I was doing it all and doing a halfway decent job at it.

The truth is, there was one thing I was not doing well. My parenting felt strained. Alcohol only made things worse. I was edgy. I was inconsistent. I was impatient.

My boys are two years apart in age. Both are strong willed and brilliant, and every day they brought me to my knees. I was exhausted. I was frustrated. The harder they were to handle, the more I looked for ways to escape. If it wasn't through booze, it was on my phone or a house project. I pined for the kids' bedtime so I could be free. I wanted autonomy. I wanted quiet. I wanted to stop being Mom for a little while and just be me again.

I knew this wasn't what parenting was supposed to be about. I'd wanted to be a mom for as long as I could remember. Why couldn't I embrace motherhood? Instead of being present with the family that I'd dreamed my whole life of having, the bottle was fogging my eyes and my perceptions.

"The days go by so fast," my friends and family would remind me every chance they got. But for me time ticked by like the slow melt of an ice cube, and I yearned for the days to speed up. I screamed at the monotony of the four walls around me, the crying kids, the depressing routine of sleep, wake, sleep, wake, sleep.

Drinking wine made time speed up. That first sip felt like redemption for my day of actionless exhaustion with seemingly nothing to show for it, a day where I did nothing but keep my kids alive and appeased, and was hopelessly and inexplicably pooped from the effort.

One night, as I polished off a glass of merlot, my then three-year-old sat next to me on the couch and watched me curiously. I stood up to refill my glass.

"Mommy, where are you going?"

"Mommy needs more wine," I huffed as I walked toward the kitchen, hearing the melancholy mix of shame and self-deprecation in my tone.

"Why, Mommy?"

I remember this moment with clarity, not because I was ready to get sober and certainly not because I was considering putting down my glass and returning to the couch. But I did ask myself, "Is this what my kids are going to remember about Mommy?" And my soul ached at the memories I was shaping for my children.

WHAT IS MOMMY WINE CULTURE?

Anyone who's been on social media in the last ten years has seen the memes: "Mommy needs wine." "I wine because my kids whine." You can buy infant onesies that say "I'm the reason mommy drinks" on Amazon.

I define Mommy Wine Culture as the social narrative that playfully jokes or implies that moms need alcohol (particularly wine) to cope with the challenges of raising children.

Mommy Wine Culture took off on our social media feeds, our store aisles, and our vernacular over the years, in an effort to laugh off the challenges of parenting. So much of motherhood is deeply messy, and some humor feels welcome, necessary even, to survive the mess. Getting a laugh out of all the wine we need to get through the day seems harmless, lighthearted, and an easy way to meld into the crowd. We are searching for connection, validation, and community. One woman commented on one of my posts that jokes about mommy and wine (I'm paraphrasing) "aren't meant to be taken at face value. It's more of a collective sigh [to] recognize parenting is really hard."

I get that. A collective sigh sounds like something we can all get behind. A collective sigh, similar to our jokes about binging Netflix after the kids go to bed. Coffee jokes because motherhood and sleep deprivation make sleep the mythical unicorn of parenthood. All of these seem like perfectly harmless collective sighs to wear like a badge of solidarity.

But I didn't see Mommy Wine Culture as all that harmless. I saw it as the reason women are drinking more than ever, as the reason we are struggling, and yes, I even saw it as the reason for my own substance misuse.

But then something surprising happened. I started researching, reading up on the history of women's drinking and drug use, as well as more background on the mental load of motherhood, and I had an epiphany: the problem with Mommy Wine Culture isn't the wine.

Yes, you read that right.

It's not about the wine. In fact, wine is just the undertone of something far more nefarious and disturbing: a cultural crush from the pressures of the mental load of motherhood, the increase in mothers returning to the workforce without appropriate support systems, and the societal expectations to do it all ourselves (and make it look easy).

This perfect storm of expectations, pressures, and lag of systematic progress has brought us here, to this time and place where we are joking about numbing out to deal with the unrealistic expectations of motherhood. A place where we are blaming our kids, schedules, and ourselves instead of recognizing the elephant in the room: we need better support. We are drowning, and some of us are doing so in the very wine bottles we've been using to survive. Mommy Wine Culture has created a self-fulfilling prophecy where, in fact, mothers need wine.

Mommy Wine Culture puts the weight of our struggles to balance home, work, and life stressors on our children.

Messages like "my kids are the reason I drink" or "my kids whine so Mommy wines" send the message to our kids that they are the problem. This is inaccurate, unfair, and damaging to our children. As a child of an alcoholic, I grew up feeling guilty and ashamed that I wasn't enough to make my father quit drinking. I can only imagine how I would have felt if he had walked around wearing a T-shirt that said, "My daughter's the reason I drink."

Maybe we are in on the joke, but are the six-year-olds who are walking the aisles with us? Do they understand this isn't supposed to be about them? Because it sure sounds like it is.

"Even if all your drinking happens after the kids go down and you're a unicorn who doesn't get hangovers that leave you dragging your feet in the morning, jokes about moms who drink can still have a negative impact on our children," says Megan Zander in an article for *Romper*.[1]

"One day, they'll be old enough to read that 'Mommy needs her wine' glass on their own, or come across the endless mom/ wine memes online," said Zander. "Jokes about needing wine to deal with parenting could lead a child to draw the conclusion that their mother needs to intoxicate herself in order to deal with them, or that they're [*sic*] something they're doing wrong in their behavior which forces their mother to drink."

Mommy Wine Culture distracts us from the real issue: getting support for mothers who are truly struggling.

A friend of mine posted about her horrible day on Facebook. Her kids were bickering, she got distracted and burned dinner, and to top it off, a client of hers called her after business hours to chew her out. "Sounds like someone needs a glass of wine . . . or three," commented someone I assume was a friend of hers. Clearly, they were trying to be funny, but it rubbed me the wrong way. I intuited that my friend was seeking connection and assurance she's a good mom (and also maybe assurance that her client was acting like a real jerk). Making light of her genuine pain was insensitive and dismissive of what might actually be a cry for help. And pointing her to a glass of wine is a far cry from offering true support.

It reminds me of the common refrain that a mom is "superhuman" for juggling so many things at once. What would happen if instead we responded, "Can I do something to help?" There's a meme from @ramblinma on Twitter that states it so perfectly.

Moms: We are drowning. Help.
Everyone: Wow you're superhuman!
Moms: What? No. Can you just hel—
Everyone: I don't know how you do it!
Moms: We're not. Help us.
Everyone: OMG you're amazing though.[2]

Praising a mom as "superhuman" or making a wine joke when someone is struggling clearly stymies someone's call for help. It's a trite way to close a conversation that could be veering far too close to vulnerable.

Mommy Wine Culture inaccurately implies that alcohol is a harmless coping mechanism when it is anything but that.

I know I said *it's not about the wine*—and it's not about wine specifically—but it is about alcohol. Studies show that no amount of alcohol is safe. The Centers for Disease Control and Prevention (CDC) now very clearly lay out the link between alcohol and six different kinds of cancer.[3] Alcohol is also extremely addictive.[4] Until we recognize this collectively as a society in the same way we have with cigarettes, mothers in particular will be inundated with the faulty, outdated message that alcohol is harmless.

WOMEN ARE THE MARKET

The proliferation of Mommy Wine Culture began in the 2010s, and with a little digging, it's not hard to see why. The continued growth in the number of women returning to work after childbirth muddled with a lag in the evolution of gender roles means women are overworked, undervalued, and unprotected.

Yet instead of calling our legislators and demanding better access to maternal health care, longer maternity leave, and more options for affordable childcare, we share jokes on the internet about mommy needing wine.

Where did the whole premise that alcohol is the solution to our parenting woes come from? Holly Whitaker, author of *Quit Like a Woman*, traces elements of Mommy Wine Culture back to tobacco marketing of the 1920s, with its newfound focus on female consumers. The tobacco industry began to introduce the idea that smoking was a means of female liberation, even calling cigarettes "torches of freedom." Over time, through influencers, advertising, and the media, the cigarette became a symbol of independence and empowerment.

Not one to miss an opportunity, Big Pharma played a critical role in marketing to women, most notably with the *mommy's little helper* of the twenty-first century.

The famous Rolling Stones song released in 1966 by that name was referring to Valium, America's most widely prescribed drug from the late 1960s to the early 1980s. Valium went on to become the pharmaceutical industry's first $100-million brand,

and according to Andrea Tone, author of *The Age of Anxiety: A History of America's Turbulent Affair with Tranquilizers*, diazepam "rapidly became a staple in medicine cabinets, as common as toothbrushes and razors."[5]

Women were the target market. By the time the earliest studies on the drug class were conducted in the 1960s, women were being prescribed Valium twice as often as men. "One of the functions of our medical system since it has organized itself has been to hand out stimulants and sedatives to American women," says David Herzberg, author of *Happy Pills in America: From Miltown to Prozac*, in an interview with *Vice*. Medical journals from around this same time depicted "viciously misogynist" cartoons of a stereotypical female patient at the doctor's office with "vague complaints" and anxieties, according to Herzberg. "It's clear that there [was] an expectation that women are mentally weak and that they're liable to have all kinds of neuroticism and anxiety."[6]

Of course, the implications of Valium did not go unnoticed for long. The US Food and Drug Administration (FDA) began imposing controls on the substance in 1967, and lawsuits over its addictive nature led to the US Justice Department ordering benzodiazepines to be classified as Schedule IV drugs in 1975, limiting refills to control access to minimize the damage that had already been done.[7]

But as the FDA limited prescriptions and put stronger guardrails around their uses, people were left to their own devices to manage anxiety, and many turned to alcohol. Alcohol was legal and considered safe to drink, even beneficial for health in moderation.

"It may be pushing it to say that alcohol is the new tobacco, but the alcohol industry is the new tobacco industry," said

Ann Dowsett Johnston, in her book *Drink: The Intimate Relationship Between Women and Alcohol.* Dowsett Johnston speaks about how Miller Brewing Company used the Philip Morris playbook to drive beer growth in the 1980s and early 1990s. "The spirits industry was seen as stodgy and boring. . . . It did market segmentation, looked at who was underperforming, and of course, it was women."[8]

In more recent years, we've seen ramped-up tactics from the alcohol industry heavily aimed at the female consumer. According to Whitaker, "Alcohol was all of a sudden an accessory to every product, service and event everywhere; wineglass holders for my bathtub, wine yoga for my nerves, pro-wine onesies for my baby, wine wands for my wine-stained teeth . . . entire Facebook pages and Instagram accounts dedicated to showcasing memes that promote binge drinking and drunkenness."[9]

"We are used to a drinking culture pitched at men . . . but Skinny Girl Vodka? Mommy Juice? When did the female drinker become the focus of the spirits market?" remarks Dowsett Johnston.[10]

The answer is easy—it was an untapped market. Big Alcohol saw an opportunity, and they took it.

Whitaker defines Big Alcohol as the consolidation of the alcohol industry to a handful of conglomerates that dominate the trade. While the alcohol industry is renowned for the money it spends on marketing, expecting to reach $6 billion in the next two years,[11] "the ace up Big Alcohol's sleeve is a woman with an Instagram account."[12] Social media enabled women, including moms, to act as influencers for Big Alcohol's goals.

So what's the big deal, right? Maybe Mommy *does* need a drink. It's just a joke, after all. I get this comment every time I write a blog post about my issue with Mommy Wine Culture. I'm also accused of shaming moms who drink, as if we moms aren't judged and shamed enough. As if instead of calling out the harm of a cultural norm, I'm directly finger wagging at any mom who feels like she needs something to take the edge off the pressure to do it all.

Why are people, especially women, so willing to defend a misogynistic marketing tactic that wants to keep women a little buzzed and too distracted to see what's really going on? We are gaslighting our own struggles and cultural misogyny with the false premise that this is something a few drinks can fix. After all, it's a hell of a lot easier to appease a woman who just wants to get loaded each night than one who's bent on fighting for equality or change.

Anne Helen Petersen, a writer who studies American culture, wisely states in an essay on today's misogyny, that perhaps instead of feeling shamed when someone calls the "mommy wine" narrative into question, "I invite you to sit with that reaction and whatever justification comes to mind—and think about where it's coming from. Why, exactly, does this thing feel defensible? And are you willing to let your feeling of vulnerability eclipse the suffering it ultimately inflicts—whether on yourself or others?"[13]

That is the point I am making here: no one is trying to take your wine glass out of your hands. The problem isn't the mom who drinks wine, it's the harm Mommy Wine Culture causes by undermining the work generations before us fought so hard for: to close the wage gap, increase our postpartum flexibility and rights, and lift the mental load of motherhood with stronger support systems. "In the past 25 years, there has been tremendous pressure on females to keep up with the guys," says David

Jernigan, director of the Center of Alcohol Marketing and Youth. "Now the industry's right there to help them. They've got their very own beverages, tailored to women. They've got their own individualized, feminized drinking culture. I'm not sure that this was what Gloria Steinem had in mind."[14]

HOW WE COPE

When I came home from the hospital with my first child, I knew I was more likely to experience postpartum depression (PPD) because I have a long, complicated history with depression. WebMD reports that most women experience "baby blues" post childbirth, and one out of ten will also experience PPD.[15] (While I am generally focused on moms here, it's worth noting that WebMD goes on to say that one out of ten fathers also experience depression in the first year after their child's birth.) What I didn't understand as a first-time parent was that depression in parenting is unique because you cannot sleep or melt away on the couch for a few weeks to focus on your recovery. Now you have a tiny human who depends on you in order to survive. Factors like sleep deprivation and the utter relentlessness of caring for a newborn intensify our feelings of desperation and confusion and deepen the challenges that come with depression. Add to the mix family and friends telling you they are *so happy* for you and suggesting, "you must be over the moon." Soon imposter syndrome comes swooping in to assure you that you don't deserve any of this and you're a terrible mother.

For moms who are in the thick of PPD or in its early stages, alcohol can be a dangerous lure (as it can for anyone struggling with depression). In less than twenty minutes, your scattered thoughts have softened, the pressure of your day melts, and your tense shoulders ease. Perhaps this hard thing isn't as hard as you make it out to be. But the effects wear off in less than an hour, and the flood of dopamine from that one glass dips, creating a rebound effect. All those good feelings you enjoyed for the past twenty to sixty minutes come at a steep price, affecting your brain and leaving you worse than before you started.[16] This is usually when folks start to reach for that second glass.

Alcohol is both a depressant and known to increase anxiety. According to Healthline, "alcohol changes levels of serotonin and other neurotransmitters in the brain, which can worsen anxiety. Alcohol-induced anxiety can last for several hours, or even for an entire day after drinking."[17] For new moms and especially moms who might be vulnerable to PPD, drinking wine is pretty much the worst suggestion you could offer. Does gifting a depressant to anyone who's just had a baby, is sleep deprived, and probably hasn't sat down for a full meal in days make sense? And yet, how often have you seen guests bring a bottle of wine to "meet the new baby" visits?

Instead of bringing along a bottle of wine, wouldn't it be more profound to offer support to parents? Or even better, offer some substantive help?

We've all heard about the proverbial village that generations past relied on to survive and thrive while raising children. The era of a true community seems to have transformed into a new era of virtual, one-dimensional Facebook moms' groups where there's often more shaming than support. And when moms do offer support in these spaces, it too often comes in the form of a joke about wine. But this "support" runs only so deep. Drinking, of course, is something you can do alone, all while still grappling with all the issues and heaviness of whatever was weighing you down in the first place.

THE BOTTOM LINE

Next time you hear me or someone else mention Mommy Wine Culture, remember: this is not an attack on moms or anyone drinking wine. This is frustration with the message that alcohol will solve some of the deeper societal woes that hold back parents, especially moms.

This isn't the first time women have been targeted with marketing and advertising to lure them away from making actual impactful progress toward gender equality. I knew this cultural playbook felt familiar, but I couldn't quite put my finger on where I'd seen it before. But when I read *Not Drinking Tonight*, by Amanda White, a licensed therapist who is in recovery for substance use disorder, it all clicked. "The root of alcohol and diet culture are the same. Both the diet and alcohol industries sell us the same idea: There is something wrong with us and they have the solution to fix us." Is it any wonder, then, that up to 46 percent of individuals with an eating disorder also experience substance use disorder at some point in their lives?[18] It's the same trap, same strategy, different pain point. But in the end, it accomplishes the same goals: to make money from women's insecurities and help distract us—weaken us even—from demanding radical, overdue systemic changes to our society. We will talk more on diet culture and other cultural scams that feed off this same patriarchal narrative in chapter three.

In 2020, the movie *Promising Young Woman* came out, starring Carey Mulligan, about Cassie, a woman who decides to hit back at the men who try to take advantage of intoxicated, vulnerable women. She pretends to be drunk at nightclubs and coyly watches men try to take advantage of her before she snaps back to stone-cold sober before their eyes and makes them pay for their atrocities. I think about how Big Alcohol is a lot like those sleezy men slinking over these seemingly weak, helpless humans, hoping to "get lucky." If only we were sober enough to see it for ourselves. If we can look past the distractions, the marketing, the subliminal messaging in advertising, we could see what Cassie saw. Big Alcohol isn't here to make friends. And when we do finally wake up to the reality of the dangers and impact alcohol has on our mental and physical health, our families, and our quality of life, there are going to be a lot of angry, sober women raising our voices and demanding societal change. And I am here for it!

PART TWO

WHY

2 | WHY I FELL INTO THE DRINKING TRAP

Growing up in a family of addiction, I saw my father squander everything for alcohol. A relatively structured, comfortable childhood would always be overshadowed by my father's drinking problem. My father was healthy, handsome, and charming and had played semiprofessional baseball before injuring his shoulder. He found success running a small business and was a natural salesman, able to wine and dine with other businessmen. He was probably a devoted fan of the renowned three-martini lunches that propagated in the 1960s and 1970s. I remember as a child often visiting his office—a small, prefabricated building in a warehouse district in Oakland, California, fascinated with the minibar in his office. In his office! "So this is what it means to be the boss," I thought.

My dad had a man cave in our home in the 1980s before man caves went mainstream. Located next to our garage, it served as a walkway to get to the rest of the house. There he kept a minifridge for his beer. His shelves were lined with dozens of trophies from his baseball days, each one bigger than the next. A pool table sat squarely in the middle, taking up most of the room. My dad spent most of his time at home in this room, watching TV and drinking beer. I have fond memories of playing pool (in the way kids often do—slamming balls against each other or jousting my siblings with the pool cues), watching my dad do pushups or plyometrics in front of his TV, or asking him for sips of his beer, which he complied with only a few times. I always thought those beers tasted like some sort of rancid spit-up anyway.

My dad sold his company for a hefty price, and suddenly he was a well-off forty-something-year-old man with a lot of time on his hands. My mom always says that's when things really went downhill. The drinking increased, the friendships became more suspicious, and the financial investments became downright alarming.

My mom, thankfully, was a working dentist at this point. She always wanted to carve her own financial path and was one of the only women in her graduating class in dental school. Through her grit and skill, we were able to keep our house and continue our comfortable lifestyle, never worrying about basic needs—even after one particularly terrible investment in a local dive bar cost my father the majority of our savings.

My mom saw the writing on the wall. She rose to the occasion and became our family's beacon of continuity and stability, while trying to maintain a demanding job that kept her largely away from home and with less control and oversight than she might have wanted. Although she started speaking to us more openly about addiction and the dangers of alcohol, she spoke in whispers, keeping our family secret just that. The pain of addiction began bleeding into the family through shame and fear.

Looking back, it seems fitting that around this time my anxiety began to rear its ugly head, and I can't help but wonder if there's a connection to the chaos that inevitably comes to a home tarnished by addiction. Intrusive thoughts about my loved ones or me dying began to consume my evenings in bed, as I tried to quell the beast of worry in my head. Darkness breeds fear, and concerns about dying, by fire or accident, or even being bombed from a plane overhead, left me in a constant state of panic.

My father was a good person—alcohol and his addiction didn't change that fact. I loved him with my whole heart. Although it took me many years to forgive the impact his drinking had on my childhood and adolescence, or on our family, I saw firsthand how hard he fought. Sadly, addiction was stronger, and no amount of pleading or threats, or even hard knocks would break the grasp alcohol held over him. It became abundantly clear how his drinking was affecting his own health when we almost lost him to a stroke at the age of fifty-two.

I was fifteen at the time. A freshman in high school. I remember the week of his stroke but not the day. Only a day or two earlier, I had forged my mom's signature to leave school early and got caught shoplifting at a local drug store. I was suspended from school, and my mom was forced to leave work to come pick me up. While the drug store, fortunately, decided not to prosecute, I had to pay a hefty (and well-deserved) fine. My actions were thoughtless, stupid, and wrong on so many levels, but the part that truly devastated me was the feeling that my actions were what sparked my father's stroke. I blamed myself well into adulthood.

Growing up in a household of addiction, one would think I would avoid alcohol with a ten-foot pole. My older sister did— she's never touched the stuff. But my thought process took a unique turn. I figured my front-row view of addiction offered me a leg up. I knew the warning signs, the danger zone, and the ramifications. I could easily avoid missteps in favor of a very healthy, pleasant life of moderation, right? Look, I know it sounds naive. But I didn't understand how something seemingly everyone else on earth seemed to consume gleefully and without incident would be my kryptonite. How unfair is that?

My family was actively involved with a nonprofit peace organization aimed at teaching children to learn about other cultures and lifestyles. When I was sixteen, I flew to Sweden for an exchange with a warm, inviting family who lived on a small farm, away from the hustle and bustle of urban living I was used to in the Bay Area. Most days we swam in the local pond with other teens or played tennis. One night, the family's sixteen-year-old daughter and I rode our bikes to a party.

I remember one of the cute local boys noticing my hands shaking as I took a glass of some sort of hard alcohol from him—probably Jägermeister, because they loved that stuff over there. My hands always shook; I have familial tremors, but I still remember my embarrassment when he pointed it out. As I sipped the drink he handed me, something incredible happened—the shakiness disappeared.

Prior to Sweden, I would sneak sips of hard alcohol with friends from my parents' liquor cabinet or occasionally drink at parties. My parents never condoned underage drinking, but they never directly told me not to either. My mom would remind me that dad was an alcoholic and that alcoholism is genetic, so watch out. But we never talked about it otherwise. I didn't understand what alcohol did, how it affected the human body, or even the dangers of losing my inhibitions after just one drink. All I really understood was that my dad drank too much, he was considered an alcoholic, but most people can drink without incident.

But something about this drink at this party provoked a feeling in me I'd never known existed. I felt beautiful, capable, and confident. My insecurities melted away. "If one drink could make me feel this good, what would two feel like?" I wondered.

I don't know how much I drank that night. My memories went blank. But the next thing I remember is a few of the girls holding me up, completely naked, in a shower. I had vomit dripping down my chest, and there was a boy just outside the bathroom asking if I was OK.

My exchange host parents came and picked us up from the party that night, leaving our bikes to be retrieved at another time. Looking back, I can only imagine the pain and terror I stirred up in those parents who had completely put their lives on hold to host me for a month. The next day we left for a nine-hour car ride to Stockholm, and it was the longest day of my life. I remember feeling so sick and worried I would puke every moment of that ride.

I stopped drinking for a while after that—most of high school in fact. If friends or people at parties asked, I would tell them my dad was an alcoholic, but the truth was I could still feel the vomit in the back of my throat during that car ride to Stockholm.

DIETS AND CONTROL

With alcohol off the table, my thoughts moved to a more tangible focus: food. I always felt overweight and disproportioned. When I was growing up, my passion was gymnastics until our recreational coach pulled my dad aside after practice one day to notify him I was "too fat for gymnastics." I was heartbroken. That moment also shifted something inside of me.

An acceptable weight felt like a condition of my happiness. Self-critical thoughts had ruled in my head before that, but to hear it from someone else created an entirely new level of identity. I started dieting in fifth grade. My mom was on the Weight Watchers point system, or sometimes she was working Jenny Craig, and she reluctantly allowed me to learn the system with her. I started to believe food was a reward, not a necessity, and that fat people weren't deserving of happiness or love. I remember bringing my WW-approved snacks to school and feeling hungry all day. My mom assured me I was just big boned, but it didn't seem fair. How did I get stuck in such an abomination of a body? Looking at the mirror made me sick. All I wanted in life was to be thin and beautiful—like Barbie or Kate Moss.

During my junior year of high school, I went on another peace exchange, this time to rural Spain. I decided to go all in on a diet and nearly stopped eating completely. By the time I returned, I was down twenty pounds, and I felt pretty good about myself. People started to notice me, compliment me even. I could buy clothes to fit a small frame, not the baggy or shapeless styles I'd worn before.

The more I got people's attention, the more I doubled down. I started counting my calories, sometimes five or six times a day. I stopped eating anything that didn't come prepackaged with the caloric content on the side. I quit the volleyball team and stopped hanging out with friends or going to parties; I didn't have the energy. Instead, I decided to focus on getting into a good college. If I could up my grades, college could be my ticket out of this nightmare called high school and life.

When I was accepted to a college outside of Boston, I felt liberated. A school on the other side of the country was just the escape I'd been hoping for. My father began attending Alcoholics Anonymous (AA) meetings, but it was just a façade—he continued drinking and tried to hide it from everyone. He fooled no one. Trips to the ER became routine, as he would fall in public or bump into things. He started hiding bottles in the bushes outside the house and would go to "check on the mail" three, four, or five times each day.

At one point I stopped speaking to him altogether. I couldn't understand how someone would choose alcohol over his own family. I remember sitting at the kitchen table with him and begging him to stop, and he looked at me dead in the eyes as he made his hand into the shape of a gun. "Bam!" he said, as he pointed his finger at his head. I realized nothing was going to stop him except death, so I stopped trying. His problem was just that—his problem—and the only thing I knew for sure was that it had nothing to do with me.

By the time I arrived at my beautiful college campus, I was at the lowest weight of my life, and I had never felt more beautiful and in control. But my energy was low and the misery of deprivation tugged at me like a girdle, so I started experimenting with purging. With practice, I found a quick and effective system, and suddenly the foods I had labeled off limits for so long became consumable again. Ice cream, cheese, and pastries. I was a kid in a candy store with every visit to the cafeteria, and eating was all I ever thought about or wanted to do.

I started drinking again in college. I was a weekend partier and drank about as much as anyone else, which, if you follow college drinking in America, is quite a lot, so I didn't stand out. If given a choice, I would have preferred to stay in my room and binge and purge. My eating disorder felt like a safety blanket from exploring "more dangerous" vices, and I felt grateful.

Approximately twenty million women in America battle an eating disorder at some point in their lives.[1] The rate of eating disorders among those who misuse alcohol or illegal drugs is eleven times higher than the rate among the general population. Likewise, people who struggle with bulimia are significantly more at risk to also misuse alcohol or other drugs at some point in their lifetime.[2]

Looking back, I think my eating disorder did protect me from developing an alcohol dependency earlier on, only in an ill-advised, "do not try this at home, kids" way. I clearly struggled with moderation, but my priorities kept alcohol on the side burner in favor of my daily bulimia.

Don't get me wrong—anyone who knew me back then would say I was a big drinker. I could out drink and outlast most, and my tolerance to alcohol was legendary—as if that's something to be proud of (which sadly, at one point I was). What many who knew me then didn't realize was that I spent countless evenings holed up in front of a toilet bowl, trying to squeeze out everything I had consumed that night: the chips, the dinner, the dessert, along with the fuzzy navels, Red Bull and vodkas, or fireball shots.

After a series of less than fantastic relationships, I met John (name changed for privacy) in my early thirties. Our relationship, as our drinking, moved fast. Drinks on dinner dates and weekends that started with mimosa brunches; alcohol served as a lubricant to dive right into a relationship I think we both knew early on was the right person at the right time. We got married within eighteen months and wanted to start having children right away.

BECOMING A MOTHER

A month after our honeymoon, a pregnancy test told us what we'd hoped to hear: we were expecting. We were giddy and more than ready, but I was also deeply afraid. This dream just got real, and there was no turning back. I immediately cut out alcohol, but the idea of going nine months without it felt daunting. John continued drinking socially, but it surprised me how easy it was for him to just opt out when he wanted. At the same time, he would offer me sips of his drinks, and I would wave him off, citing the baby in my belly. But secretly, what I never told anyone is that I was less afraid of taking a sip of alcohol than of not being able to stop.

Since childhood, I've known I wanted to be a mother. I dreamed of finding love, then being pregnant, and, finally, holding a child of my very own. I was fairly certain that the answers to many of my questions about life, purpose, and meaning would be answered when I had children. And some were: I have found so much beauty and depth in the miracle of my children. But other things I expected to show up naturally at my front door when I arrived home with our first child, Kevin (name changed for privacy), didn't make an appearance.

Mommy intuition was one of them. We brought Kevin home after two nights at the hospital, and he seemed distraught from the moment we walked through the front door, screaming incessantly and acting nothing like the docile, sleepy baby from the hospital. I remember calling the maternity ward that same day in tears, waving the white flag after less than six hours on my own. "Something is wrong; he isn't responding to anything we try!" I secretly hoped they would say, "Come back in, your bed is still here." Of course, they assured us this was normal baby behavior and we would soon find a groove.

But finding a groove with little Kevin was easier said than done. He showed significant signs of colic and would projectile vomit after every feeding. John and I would spend hours trying to soothe him or get him to sleep, only to have him awaken easily with just a shift in positioning or the ever-challenging transition from my arms to the crib.

Fear that I couldn't soothe my own child or instinctively interpret his needs weighed heavily on me, as did the terrible sleep and tremendous fear and intrusive thoughts that I already suspected to be the beginning of PPD.

I called my OB to cite my concerns. Her response left me dismayed. "If you are having thoughts about harming yourself or your baby, you need to go to the psych ward," she said coolly. "Otherwise, it will work itself out, and there's nothing we can do about it."

I was shocked. Admit myself to a psychiatric hospital or just suck it up? That was my choice? I was struggling, but nothing was going to tear me away from my baby. I quickly downplayed my symptoms but made a mental note that people were watching me carefully now. Anything I said or did could potentially be used to rip me from my child. My guard was up, and I vowed to play my cards close to my chest from then on. There was too much at stake and too much to lose.

At my mom's encouragement, I cautiously opened up about some of my PPD symptoms to a new OB, who took me seriously and treated me with grace. She prescribed an antidepressant and assured me that I would start to feel better soon, and I did.

We had regular visitors in the early days of being home with our new baby. Many people came to meet our son and bring us dinners and alcohol to celebrate our new arrival. "You'll need this" was a common refrain as folks would hand over champagne, wine, or even hard liquor. Now that I was no longer pregnant, I was eager to understand the rules of engagement around drinking again. I'd seen the "mommy needs wine" memes that littered social media, offering some solace after a long day of spit-ups and diaper changes, and I was eager to be in on the joke.

I started pouring one glass with dinner, timed diligently after breastfeeding, which slowly progressed to several throughout the evening while I learned the pump-and-dump game. I purchased Milkscreen testers on Amazon, and with a quick dip of a tester in a freshly pumped bottle of breast milk, I could easily determine if my milk was alcohol free.

With time, I learned just about every trick in the "breastfeed-and-still-drink" playbook, thanks to dozens of Google searches and mommy blogging forums. I moderated my drinking fairly well, just as I'd planned. I was a "responsible" mommy, and responsible mommies know when they've had enough.

I grandly announced an end to breastfeeding when my son was ten months old, timed perfectly with a vacation to Mexico. I had no interest in carting my hospital-grade breastfeeding pump across the border, and besides, breastfeeding was exhausting. I also hadn't started menstruating again, and we were hoping to start trying for a second child right away.

I realized pretty quickly that heavy drinking and parenting do not mix. In fact, science shows that the hell known as hangovers doubles in severity if you have to parent small children the next day (kidding . . . no study has been done on this, but I wouldn't be surprised if those were the findings).

Something else started happening once I was a mom back on the booze train, scarier than a hangover. My anxiety spiked like I had never felt before. Things that never had bothered me, like driving on the freeway or going on a ski lift, sent me into a panic. Even though I was trying to be cautious with my consumption, parenting while trying to live my old lifestyle of regular drinking did me zero favors.

After an early miscarriage, John and I got pregnant with Ben (name changed for privacy). I knew in my heart this would be my last everything: last pregnancy, last belly kicks, last endless hiccups from within. I soaked it all in, and the days flew by so much faster the second time, as we were also chasing around Kevin.

Our time after Ben was born was the polar opposite of our experience with Kevin. Ben was so mellow, so calm. He slept well, ate well, and was a model of what people must mean when they say a baby's "easy." He made me feel like a good, confident mother, and I started to think maybe I'd finally gotten this motherhood thing figured out.

When Kevin was three, we enrolled him at a local private preschool we'd heard really good things about. That was when we started to receive feedback about atypical behavior. Words like *aggression* and *opposition* started to show up frequently in the messages we received from his teacher.

When we spoke with Kevin's pediatrician, though, he was unconcerned. "These behaviors are fairly normal in children at this age," he said with confidence. "If it's something that continues in the next few years, we can run some tests."

Did he actually expect us to wait this out for the next few years? I was just trying to get through each day! I had been a compliant, people-pleasing child myself, so this whole "going to the principal's office" thing around Kevin's behavior was way out of my comfort zone. I felt fearful and helpless, and I needed to know what to do now—not in a few years. We didn't know if these were early indications of neurodivergence or just a child maturing at a slower pace, but the idea of not doing anything sent me into a panic. I wanted to address these questions right away, not sit on them with a "wait and see" approach.

The pediatrician said something next that struck me as interesting enough to heed but still didn't create a light bulb moment. He said that kids with these kinds of behavioral challenges thrive on routine. The more structure and consistency we could provide him, the better he'd do. I held onto that advice and focused on creating the best routine and schedule Kevin had ever seen. Subconsciously I believe I knew that making some personal changes of my own could give my son a consistent environment that would truly help him succeed; something that was missing in my own childhood.

That November, my husband began showing signs of depression. It ran in his family, and when he'd experienced it in the past, we'd dealt with it, but now it left me panicked. He was doing the best that he could to be an active part of the family, but he felt lethargic and had rapid mood swings. I knew the drill: he would need time and therapy, and my main concern would be taking care of the children. What worried me most was how we would give Kevin the consistency he needed when I couldn't count on his dad right then for support.

MY LIGHT BULB

I don't know how much I was drinking at that point, but it was enough to be concerned. I remember attending church one day and feeling drawn to the prayer request forms that filled the cubbies of the seats in front. I wrote down, "I am sabotaging everything good in my life," and I passed the card in. I wasn't even sure what it meant at the time, but I felt like this spiral staircase I was slowly walking down was turning into a full-on slide and was picking up speed. Something would need to change.

And change it would. Things came to a head one cold, bland December Monday at work when out of the blue, I started struggling to breathe. A cold sweat washed over me. Something felt very wrong. I drove to the emergency room, fearful that I was having a stroke just like my father. I'll tell more of this story later in the book, but by the time the doctor had run his tests and concluded I'd experienced a panic attack, I knew what came next. I knew it like I knew I needed to quit drinking the day the pregnancy tests came back positive. I needed to end my relationship with alcohol. I was putting myself on a path of self-destruction and would lose everything if I didn't make this change right now.

As I drove home that day, I mourned like I had lost a loved one, and I felt like I'd failed. I'd taken the "adulting" test and hadn't passed. I would be doomed to misery for the rest of my life, stuck sipping bubble water while everyone else lived their best liquored-up lives. It was one of the hardest days of my life, and it felt like the end of all things grand and enjoyable.

Looking back though, I can't help but feel tremendous gratitude for that day at the ER. It was finally the light bulb moment I was waiting for; it was the bug in my ear from Kevin's pediatrician and that day at church. It was realizing I couldn't make my husband do the heavy lifting and recognizing for the first time that change had to start with *me*.

Looking back, I give myself grace for the tears, the fear, and the anger of that day. Because I can now call it my Day 1.

PART THREE

HOW

3 | THE MENTAL LOAD WE CARRY

SARAH'S STORY

Sarah, forty-four, reached out to me after I went public with my sobriety on social media. Our paths often crossed at networking events and in business. She always struck me as so on top of things, truly a type-A personality who you could count on to get the job done.

When we met for lunch, she told me she respected my choice to go public with my sobriety, but then she surprised me with a question: "How did you quit?"

As we dug deeper in the conversation, I learned that this successful, powerful woman carving a respectable path in our local business community secretly knew she'd lost control over her alcohol use. Unlike me, she didn't see any gray area in her drinking. She was certain she had a drinking problem. She'd attended AA, gone to sober retreats, and spoken to her husband about her struggles. She told me she could get months of not drinking under her belt but always fell back to old patterns.

"How are we expected to 'wine and dine' clients without wine?" we mused together in between bites of salad and sips of seltzer with lime. It had taken Sarah years to earn a seat at the power table with the heavy hitters and decision makers, and drinking was, and is, a big part of that scene.

The work drinking culture is hugely influential in many businesses. The expectation to work hard, play hard is fun and exciting until you get back to your hotel room, alone and drunk, left to lick your wounds before an early-morning meeting the next day, and that's the best-case scenario. I've heard other nightmares of people hooking up with a colleague, saying something inappropriate to a boss, or revealing confidential information to a client, all while deeply inebriated.

Add the mental load of motherhood to that, and we're often left feeling overwhelmed, overstretched, and compelled to juggle all the plates and make it look effortless for fear of being overlooked for the next promotion. Certain that without that effort we'll be taken off the high-achiever list and relegated to the "she's lost her passion for work" club because (gasp!) she values her family more than her job.

Sarah knew what she had to do. She'd made the decision mentally years before that sobriety was the only option for her, but she felt stuck in a very toxic work culture that pulled her back in again and again.

Sarah's story reminds me that alcohol often overpowers the strongest, highest achievers. That the pressure to drink in work and social settings can override any sensible effort to take care of ourselves. People determined to build careers and friendships could be especially susceptible to addiction if drinking dovetails with being seen as a team player, and helps to numb any doubts as they keep reaching toward success. But those people also represent incredible beacons of hope in recovery. It's exactly that tenacity and determination that drives their transformation and growth. And I see that in Sarah; I see her strength and I can tell that her sober journey is just getting started.

Excerpt from my blog

May 30, 2020

"You're in charge of dinner," I told my mom last night. I was just so tired. I recently started a new job and the learning curve was exhausting. All that topped with listening to my kids screaming downstairs all day, while I worked in my bedroom, left me mentally drained in a way that I never felt pre-COVID.

"OK," my mom responded. "Should I give the kids mac and cheese? Fish sticks? Do both the kids like fish sticks?"

I pretended not to hear her as I walked upstairs. By delegating dinner to her, her question was exactly what I wanted a break from. It wasn't just the actual cooking and setting the table, finding out which kid wants milk and which wants water. Then the power struggle of how much they each needed to eat to warrant dessert, followed by clean up. It's the mental load of making decisions. Of running the household. Of being in charge of everything.

Where is my green dinosaur?

Are the dishes in the dishwasher dirty?

Do we have any toilet paper?

When's the last time the bed sheets were cleaned?

Do the kids have their dentist appointments scheduled? Doctor? When does soccer season start and will it conflict with play therapy?

This is the mental load of motherhood. I am in charge of all of it. I store it all in my head, and yes, I have the answers to all of it. But sometimes, I wish I didn't. Sometimes, I wish I could pass the buck.

Check the dishwasher yourself. Where did you last see your dinosaur? Did you check the garage for more toilet paper?

But for the most part, the reason the weight of the mental load is so heavy, is because I do know. I do know where you left your dino. I do know the dishes in the dishwasher are clean, and probably still hot, so be careful when touching them. I know it's been more than a week since the bed sheets were cleaned and yes, I know when every appointment is scheduled and where we are on the IEP.

And the paradox of it all? I want to know. I want to be in charge 95% of the time. I wouldn't have it any other way . . . must be the controller in me. But it's that last 5% that gets me every time. It's the part that makes me snap and yell, often passive aggressively ask, "Have you looked?" or ignore the questions and walk away. Because that 5% just wants to mute all the noise. Tune out everyone else and focus on me. Me—not me as a mom, a wife, an employee—just me as a person. Because, sometimes, she gets so lost in the chaos, I'm not ever sure she's still there.

I should mention my mom took the hint. She figured dinner out and gave me time to sit with myself, alone and undisturbed. When I did come back down, I felt refreshed and ready to resume my duties. I asked my mom how much the kids ate and where the kids were on the dessert trajectory. I was back. My 5% was filled. I was ready to mom again.

As moms, we don't always get this time. Sometimes we don't get any break, as single moms know all too well. But maybe, by explaining to our partners and family, that we need to fill our 5% . . . maybe they can better understand. Last night wasn't just about cooking dinner for the family, it was about making the decisions around it, too. Those decisions can be heavy.

The mental load is something we carry as mothers. It is heavy. Yes, moms have superpowers. We can carry heavy. We do it all the time. But as humans, we eventually need to put it down.

The learning curve around caring for a new baby is steep—perhaps steeper than anything I've encountered, because it always feels like everything is on the line.

Trying to learn how to keep a baby alive is a job in and of itself. I had finally gotten the hang of breastfeeding. My body had finally healed. My colicky son was finally starting to slow down his constant wailing. We were only waking up to feed him a few times a night at this point. But only six weeks after he was born, it was time to go back to work, and life got upended all over again. Now I had to learn how to hand my baby to a stranger at day care. I had to pack up frozen bags of milk and make sure day care had a constant supply. I would get to work with my pump and set my timer every two hours, except for lunch when I would drive over to the school on my break to breastfeed while I ate. Yes. While. I. Ate. While little crumbs fell on my son's head as he latched on to me for dear life.

Then I would scramble back to work, pretending I didn't just leave a piece of me back at day care while I fumbled through meetings and emails and squared away in my head what on earth we would have for dinner that night. Eventually I would get home to a laundry pile the size of Kilimanjaro, an empty pantry, and a hungry husband who also just spent the day away at work. I was ready to explode. Or implode. Or just hop the first flight to Hawaii—alone. I needed help, I needed changes, and I needed to understand how I got here.

THE MENTAL LOAD

While the concept of the mental load and emotional labor has been around for years (emotional labor was first defined by

47

sociologists in 1983),[1] the modern application of the concept, which has gained visibility in recent years, incorporates cognitive labor, emotional labor, and mental labor[2] along with the impact of that labor on relationships. It refers to the responsibility of parenting and household duties, in addition to organizing, reminding, and planning for the family.[3] Most of the time, it's a responsibility that falls squarely on the woman's shoulders in heterosexual cisgender partnerships, as tradition and gender roles have primarily connected women to these duties. But when maternity leave is over (assuming there was one) and the load doesn't shift more onto the other partner in the relationship—traditionally a father, but any partner if there is one—that's where things start to get dicey.

Suddenly, a mom with a new baby isn't just returning to work—she's adding that to her roles as mom, CEO of the household, activity organizer, buyer/wrapper of holiday and birthday gifts, wedding RSVPer, and babysitter scheduler. So yes, it's called mental load for a reason.

Gemma Hartley takes it one step further. In her book, *Fed Up: Emotional Labor, Women, and the Way Forward*, she speaks to the emotional labor we carry in these positions, defining "emotional labor" as "emotion management and life management combined. It is the unpaid, invisible work we do to keep those around us comfortable and happy. It is work that is mentally absorbing and exhausting, and emotional labor has repercussions that follow us into the world."[4]

It's more than just laundry and calendar management. It's keeping the family functional and yes, happy, so the kids are more likely to have a good day at school. It's keeping mental tabs on scheduling visits to the pediatrician, buying a gift for Grandma's birthday, and who's babysitting next Saturday so we can go to the holiday party.

My husband and I had a frank conversation a few months into our new roles as parents. I explained to him that I was drowning. Drowning in my self-imposed expectation that nothing would need to change in our routines, housework, and professional work structure post baby.

It felt wildly unfair that I bore the brunt of the responsibility of a child we both conceived and desperately wanted. I didn't understand how my life felt completely upended and his seemed to fall back into place relatively smoothly. I couldn't adjust to a new baby, the doctor visits, recovering from a traumatic birth that quite literally ripped my vagina open, constant nursing and pumping, and carrying on my job and household expectations as if it were just another day.

That night we divvyed up the responsibilities more equally. My husband was happy to be more involved—frankly he didn't understand why I hadn't asked sooner. Besides, the times he did try to help or pitch in, I could be dismissive or cold. My constant need to control the schedule, the environment, and the outcome left him feeling dismissed or like he was in the way, a prime example of communication challenges and misunderstandings that come up in parenting and can be worked through.

We switched off night feedings and started looking at incorporating formula into the baby's feeding routine to lessen my constant worry about supply of breast milk. He started taking our son to day care in the morning and doing grocery runs on his way home.

We did not reallocate the mental load of motherhood overnight. Not even close. But we started the conversation, which made all the difference, and more than anything, it made me feel seen and heard, which is a precious feeling when a child enters the world and you start to lose sight of where your needs end and your baby's needs begin.

There's a fantastic YouTube video about a magic coffee table. I encourage you to Google it. In it, a British couple stand in front of a coffee table as the man goes on and on about how the coffee table is magic. "Anything you leave on this coffee table just vanishes overnight," he excitedly shares with her, as she fumes with contempt. Later, when he's talking to the police about his wife going missing, presumably because she left out of spite after all the invisible work she's done over the years that went unacknowledged, the policeman says he has that same "magic" coffee table at home. This is obviously a parody, but it speaks to the burden many women carry in the household, often without their partner realizing, or at least acknowledging.

And while, yes, it's gotten better over the years—dads are more involved in family life than ever—we are far from balanced. Hartley states, "The amount of time spent on housework more than doubled for fathers between 1965 and 2015, and the amount of time spent on childcare nearly tripled, but these leaps and bounds haven't brought us to full equality. The gender gap at home persists in a big way. Women are still spending double the time men do on both domestic labor and caring for children. . . . Even when there is a fifty-fifty split in domestic labor and childcare, we aren't qualifying the emotional labor that goes into these tasks."[5]

I remember more recently we were packing up the car to go to a friend's birthday party. I had bought the gift weeks ago and wrapped it the night before. As we started pulling out of the driveway, I screamed, "We forgot the gift!" My toddler snapped right back, "Mom, *you* forgot the gift." Touché. I wanted to wail, because wow that was heartless, and damn it, he was technically right. Because the mental load is a thankless, painful weight to carry that only gets noticed when something goes wrong.

It's no wonder that the term "emotional labor" is often coupled with "invisible work," because the majority of what helps the family and the day run smoothly all too often remains unnoticed when everything goes according to plan.

People tell you your marriage will change after the baby. People tell you sex slows down, date nights are hard to come by, and communication can be challenging. No one mentions the mental load. Not one book of the half dozen I'd read on having a baby brought up the necessary conversations you must have with your partner about changing roles and responsibilities once there's a child in the house—and then must have again if the mother goes back to work, then again when each new life change enters the picture, often flying in like a wrecking ball.

I included in this chapter the conversation I had with my husband for a few reasons. Whether it's in writing, a long talk, an all-hands-on-deck team huddle, even a big fight—it's a conversation I think every new parenting couple has—or should have— on some level. The mental load of motherhood is perhaps the most overlooked stressor of early parenting today. It's the root of enormous discontent, fear of failure, and loneliness. But it doesn't have to be. It is something that through communication, openness, and the life-changing gift of couples counseling, we can overcome this common breaking point for new parents.

But we don't know what we don't know. In my own relationship, while that very first conversation about our shared responsibilities was revelatory, it didn't solve everything. In fact, we've had to have this conversation over and over again. We would bicker, hold grudges, then come to an understanding and make amends—until the next round. This happened countlessly, after our firstborn and later after our second. But of course, I couldn't see into the future. I didn't know after each dip of this relationship roller coaster, internally I was building up resentment, anxiety, and internal strife, negativity that would only let go when we made changes to balance our family responsibilities more evenly.

I want to stop for a moment to recognize that for single parents, the mental load basically has nowhere else to go. The weight of that labor stays firmly planted on the shoulders of a sole caretaker. Especially now, when the notion that it takes a village to rear kids has urban legend status, nobody has a harder road than a single parent who has virtually no one to help, no place to set down some of that burden. Black and other marginalized single mothers face an even greater hurdle: in addition to the usual single parent challenges, they also often experience stigmatization and systemic racism that can be rooted within their own community—a system they also must teach their children to navigate safely.

In an article for the *Huffington Post*, single mom and postgraduate student Rochelle Rodney says, "I had . . . inherited the deep-seated social stigmas that paint single mothers as unstable, shameful, and poverty-stricken. As a woman, I am forced to make choices in life that are more costly than those of men; such as choosing children over a career. As a Black woman, these weighty choices feel even more stark knowing the old adage that, because I am Black, I have to work twice as hard to get half as far."[6]

THE MOST IMPORTANT JOB

In *Fed Up*, Hartley says, "Our culture lauds motherhood, holds it up as 'the most important job a woman can have,' then does little to nothing to support us (just look at the outlandish cost of childcare) and admonishes us when we fail to do the job as expected—even when we are going it alone."[7]

I returned to work after six weeks of unpaid time off. Because the company I worked for had less than fifty employees, they were not required by law to give me any time off. The fact that I had a job to come back to at all was by the grace of my boss—which he made sure to tell me directly.

Parenting a new baby is hard enough. Carrying the mental load doubles that weight. Trying to manage both on little sleep and returning to work? That's just crazy. But it's the reality for most of us. A study by PEW Research Center cites that 73 percent of American women return to work in six months or less after childbirth.[8] Besides Papua New Guinea, the United States is the only country in the world that does not mandate any paid leave for new mothers under federal law, though a few states do require it under state law.[9] Only 19 percent of workers have access to any sort of paid maternity leave through their employers.[10] This vastly differs from 194 of our counterparts, with countries such as Bulgaria, Greece, and the United Kingdom offering thirty-nine or more weeks of full and partial pay.[11]

According to the US Census Bureau's 2018 American Community Survey, working mothers contributed to a significant part of the labor force, accounting for nearly one-third (32 percent) of all employed women.

The census counted 23.5 million employed women with children under the age of eighteen, with nearly two-thirds of them working full time, year-round.[12]

The rise in the number of working mothers over the years has increased the mental load of motherhood. Job responsibilities mixed with those for family and home life contribute to the pressure and challenges that leave women feeling overwhelmed and incapable. The myth of work/life balance fed to us by high-achieving "you can do it" media personalities and social media influencers, who assert that there's enough time to do everything on your checklist, that you can be everything to all people and still be home in time for family dinner (hell, to make family dinner!), and the only thing stopping you is your mindset, just furthers the burnout among moms.

Then, of course, there's the COVID-19 pandemic, which sent everyone into quarantine in 2020. Suddenly, kids were sent home from school, or, as happened in our school district, they never returned to in-person classes after spring break. I was between jobs, trying to get to the root cause of some of the neurological delays we were seeing in Kevin. He was in kindergarten, and I was in communication with the principal and teachers daily hoping to find a structure and support that worked for him. We'd begun attending free parenting classes through the school district and working with several specialists. But all of this took time. I couldn't schedule the appointments, take classes, and field the phone calls from school while holding down a full-time job. Not to mention the impact these concerns had on my own mental health, as my anxiety spiked and I started to feel triggered to drink. The proliferation of alcohol memes (quarantinis and pandemic punch, anyone?) and jokes about drinking before noon flooded my social media feed; apparently a pandemic is justification to throw health rules out the window. As one person tweeted: "I don't know who needs to hear this but, Quarantine Rules are Airport Rules, have a drink at 9am [sic] if you want to."[13]

So when our kids didn't return to school at all after break, it was obvious that I'd be leading the homeschooling along with support from my now-retired mom. It just made sense, since I was already home anyway. Unlike many couples we know, my husband and I didn't have to make the hard decision if one job should be sacrificed, or how to balance between us these new responsibilities.

I was in the minority, however, as the COVID-19 pandemic hit working mothers hard. According to the census bureau, "The pandemic has had a devastating effect on employment overall but especially on mothers' paid labor. The 10 million not working accounted for over one-third of all mothers living with school-age children in the United States."[14]

Census bureau data further shows that mothers were more significantly hurt by the economic implications of the pandemic than fathers, for two main reasons: (1) mothers are more likely to be working in service jobs and other professions that were more widely impacted by pandemic closures; and (2) mothers carry a heavier burden of the unpaid domestic household chores and childcare. The fact that the pandemic forced everyone to be within the confines of home disrupted a parent's ability to work for pay.[15]

In an article for the trade magazine *PR Week*, Anne Colaiacovo recounted a name given to the economic phenomenon affecting women during the pandemic. "Women's labor-force participation reached a thirty-three-year low in January 2021, putting us in what economists have dubbed a 'shecession.' In addition to the millions of women who left the workforce, millions more barely hold on and find their mental health at a tipping point. The idea of not giving your family the attention they deserve, never fully being able to step away from work, not doing enough, and not being a competent employee have created increased feelings of guilt and neglect. The pressures from every direction have built extreme levels of anxiety and stress, which has led to a complete mental overload and left working mothers feeling overburdened and undersupported."[16]

In a heartfelt post on her website, Revolution from Home, writer Beth Berry wrote a viral essay called "Dear Mothers: We Can't Keep Pretending Like This Is Working for Us." In it, she bluntly argues, "Modern-day motherhood in the US (and many other developed countries) is not just stressful and overwhelming. It's giving birth to a whole new form of oppression comprised of cultural norms and narratives that set mothers up to feel disempowered and inadequate and make our thriving extremely difficult."[17]

Berry connects the lack of postpartum support, untenable parenting standards, costs of childcare, and lack of benefits as a web that sets us up to fail, or at least keeps us down. Ultimately, it forces many mothers to choose between staying home to raise their child or working full time, not because they want one more than the other but because they have no other choice. Perhaps the cost of childcare exceeds or is equal to your salary, forcing you to decide if it's better to stay home but risk the "mommy gap," the expression for an employment gap in your résumé.

Women are more overwhelmed than ever. The mental load for mothers is at an all-time high, and it's hard to see any reprieve in sight.

"Seventy-eight percent of moms say they are so busy maintaining family stability by being constantly available mentally and physically, to deal with every detail of home life that they aren't taking care of themselves,"[18] says Eve Rodsky, author of *Fair Play*. What are we doing instead?

Well, many of us are drinking. "In many women's lives, we miss the biggest part of the story if we don't link drinking to the issue of self-medication," said Dowsett Johnston. "It's an all-too-common reality in modern society: using alcohol for what ails us."

A little over a year before I quit drinking, I wrote a piece for Scary Mommy aptly titled "I'm a Mom Who Self-Medicates, and It's Complicated": "So, on the days when going to bed at 7:30 isn't an option, sometimes I break out a wine glass instead. The best part is I can enjoy the wine and feel like I'm treating myself, while still getting my obligations done at the same time. Self-medicating? Boo. But multitasking? Hooray! It feels even better because I'm not being completely selfish and directing all my time and attention on me and relaxation. It feels like something a responsible mom who wants to wind down would do."[19]

Looking back on my words, I'm saddened at how little I knew or understood about the impact my drinking was having on my daily medications to treat anxiety and depression. I did not understand that alcohol was a depressant and possibly neutralizing, even hampering, any positive impacts of my medication. Nor did I realize the dangers, risks, or increased side effects when mixing alcohol with SSRIs commonly prescribed to treat anxiety and depression[20]—drugs I've been taking most of my adult life.

It's hard not to speak to the impact of the mental load of motherhood and not also connect the disproportionate number of women who struggle with anxiety and depression compared to men. Women are twice as likely to suffer from anxiety as men and 70 percent more likely to experience depression,[21] and while brain chemistry and hormone fluctuations are believed to play a key role,[22] the additional stress women carry in a still very patriarchal society looms large. If women are bearing the brunt of the family responsibilities in a household, then it makes sense that their anxiety will be higher. And, for many of us, the drinking makes it worse.

During the pandemic, I reconnected with Gemma Hartley. We'd met years before as fellow writers when we learned we both live in Reno and frequent the same yoga studio. I watched her article for *Harper's Bazaar*, "Women Aren't Nags—We're Just Fed Up," explode with more than two billion views.[23] And I sat in a row just behind her kids during her local reading of her book on the subject, *Fed Up*. We've texted back and forth ever since, and she even helped me research and pitch my agent. When she publicly announced she was six months sober, I was especially excited to talk to her for this book.

Gemma sighed in frustration when we started chatting about how much the pandemic impacted our lives and the expectation right from the start that women would do the heavy lifting. Wouldn't this have been the perfect opportunity for us as a society to make impactful, immediate changes to positively benefit women? she wondered. "And then nothing changed. That was the thing, nothing changed. If we had any intention to fix things and to change the way that the world works, it would have happened by now. [Instead] we just let that opportunity pass."

"What I decided was that if no one's coming to save us, then I need to create a life that didn't need saving. I just reevaluated the way that I wanted to live my life. I want to do things that I'm passionate about, I want to stop doing the things that make me feel like crap, which is why I finally decided that I was going to quit drinking."[24]

Gemma's frustrations mirrored my experience. In early motherhood, wine seemed a quick and effective cure for my frustrations, my mental load, and my fears that I couldn't keep going on this way.

I thought that maybe as a mother my relationship with alcohol would be different. I could learn how to moderate my drinking, and it would be the start of something fresh and special. Slow and controlled. It didn't occur to me that as my tolerance built, I started needing more wine to get the same effect. Upping my pour and eventually opting for another glass felt natural, necessary even. According to Joseph Nowinski, PhD and author of *Almost Alcoholic*, "Drinking has a tendency to escalate—one glass turns into two and then three."[25] It would take years before I realized what was really happening. By the time I reached a bottle a night, it didn't feel dangerous at all. It felt like I was completely in control.

SIMILAR SCHEMES THAT DISEMPOWER WOMEN

A 2017 study sponsored by the National Institute on Alcohol Abuse and Alcoholism found that between 2001 and 2013, the prevalence of alcohol use among women in the United States rose close to 16 percent. During the same time frame, the percentage of women who have four or more drinks on a given day on a weekly basis rose by 58 percent.[26]

And the pandemic has only made things worse. According to a RAND Corporation study, during the pandemic women have increased their heavy drinking days by 41 percent compared to before the pandemic. "It's a perfect drug for women in particular, in a lot of ways," Sarah Hepola, author of *Blackout: Remembering the Things I Drank to Forget*, said in an interview with ABC News. "Makes you feel braver, empowered, strong, it's a pain management system—and it's a forgetting drug, and a lot of us are in a place where we just don't want to think a lot right now. And as far as women go right now, a lot of them are bearing the biggest burden of dealing with both work and added domestic stresses, homeschooling, childcare, keeping the household from falling apart. A glass of wine or two, 'mother's little helper,' that's socially acceptable."[27]

There's a clear correlation between the rise in women's drinking and the mental load of motherhood. The wine memes that jam our social media pages are only communicating what women have been trying to convey for years: we are exhausted, we are overwhelmed, we are overworked, and we are in serious need of a major shift in cultural expectations, working moms' services, coping strategies, and *help*—above all else.

But alcohol isn't the only industry that feeds off women's struggles. I promised you in chapter one I would connect the dots on Mommy Wine Culture and other ways we deflect women's grievances, so let's get to it.

As I was writing this book, I started to see more parallels to similar messages that were gaslighting women into believing our struggles were individual, humorous (mommy needs wine is a joke, after all), and nothing a few drinks couldn't fix. Sounds familiar, doesn't it? But in what way?

Then I started to think about the pervasive messaging we hear—from other mothers, no less—about ways to "fix" our challenges. Sheryl Sandberg's Lean In movement, Rachel Hollis's toxic positivity, the multilevel marketing (MLM) industry that saw a huge opportunity in "boss babe" mindset to encourage female liberation while girl bossing directly off our credit cards— "shop from your own store . . . be a product of the product"—all MLM jargon used to bank big money with consultants, and a behemoth of industries that target women—diet and beauty culture. After all, aren't we all just ten to fifteen pounds and a Botox injection away from living the life of our dreams?

Whoa, that's a lot all at once, so let's break this down a little.

The Lean In movement, a phenomenon started by Sheryl Sandberg that encouraged women to "lean in" to the patriarchal, antiquated work systems of the eight-to-five, leave your kids with a caretaker all day, and hire a housekeeper (I exaggerate here, but not by much), sent an extremely unrealistic message to women that any sort of barriers (physical, mental, or financial) to breaking through the glass ceiling rest on our individual shoulders. "Sandberg's message was often distilled to its simplified, can-do essence: If a woman works hard enough, and asserts herself enough, she can thrive at home and at work," Caitlin Gibson writes in an article for the *Washington Post*.[28] Messages like Sandberg's suggest that it's not a systemic issue, but that a personal change in priorities will help you have it all. But let's face it—having a lot of money isn't going to hurt here.

"I tell women, that whole 'you can have it all'—nope, not at the same time; that's a lie," Michelle Obama famously said in 2018. "It's not always enough to lean in, because that shit doesn't work."[29]

Gibson's article goes on to say "certain aspects of Sandberg's self-empowerment philosophy haven't aged well: research shows that pervasive issues—such as gender-based pay inequality, the disproportionate burden of domestic responsibilities on women, and the number of US companies offering paid family leave—remain largely unchanged."[30] And the issue of racial and socioeconomic barriers are all but unspoken in this laughably simplified message that women can achieve their professional goals through shifting priorities, demanding raises, and a "will to lead" (taken from the book's subtitle).

Another cultural movement that gaslighted women's collective grievances was the toxic positivity, hustle culture from books like *Girl Wash Your Face* or *Girl, Stop Apologizing*, by Rachel Hollis. This watered down "you can do it" message exploded in the 2010s by encouraging women to believe they simply need to get out of their own damn way to make their dreams come true. "At the center of Hollis's messaging is the conviction that if you simply 'choose positivity,' you can change the material conditions of your life to become a happier, more fulfilled being," says Amanda Arnold in an opinion piece on The Cut. "She lays out this principle in the intro of *Girl, Wash Your Face*: 'You, and only you, are ultimately responsible for how happy you are.'"[31]

In a blog post I shared on Facebook on how the hard parts of motherhood are rarely acknowledged, a commenter shared, "I posted a rant on Facebook . . . and at the very end I literally posted . . . 'just let me rant.' And the very first comment on my post? 'Focus on the positive.' You're either ignored or you're told you're wrong for sharing your negative feelings. And it hurts either way."

And what's worse? We know better. Toxic positivity is scientifically shown *not* to help us improve our mindset or situation. Instead, it leads to feelings of denial, minimization, and invalidation of our authentic and perfectly normal human emotional experiences.[32]

In a piece written for the Women's Opportunity Center, a nonprofit dedicated to work-readiness programs for those facing barriers to gaining or retaining employment, Julia Dath says "Hustle culture . . . puts feminism on an individual lens, purporting the idea that an individual person working harder is the way to overcome gender stereotypes and barriers in workplace environments. In other words, if I work hard and push my way through sexist structural barriers and misogyny in the workplace, I can succeed. The problem is that pushing my way to the top does not dismantle the structures that work against women in the first place. It leaves them intact and fully functional to disenfranchise other women."[33]

I would be remiss not to mention an industry that also feeds off mothers' weaknesses and this hustle culture mindset: MLMs. As a former #bossbabe myself, who talked myself into an MLM not once but twice, I too fell for the idea that I could fit network marketing "into the 'nooks and crannies of my life.'" I believed that if I could find success selling my soul (COUGH—I mean skin care and protein shakes) to my friends and family, I could quit my day job and have the work-life balance I dreamed of. Except that I was spending far more money buying products to use, sample to potential customers, and gift than I was making and desperately posting my picture-perfect life on social media in hopes of recruiting people to my team. It eventually exploded in my face when I almost lost a best friend and created discord in my family after pressuring them too much. And over what—protein powder?

Emily Paulson, author of the book *Hey Hun: Sales, Sisterhood, Supremacy, and the Other Lies Behind Multi-Level Marketing*, says MLMs and alcohol marketing are similar in that they all tie back to the same key issues for mothers: isolation and being overworked. "We offer women alcohol as band aids. And we are going to commodify all the things you hate about yourself (your body, your face, your health). We are going to sell you something under the guise of sisterhood and women's liberation. It's all very insidious."[34]

Then there's the health and wellness industry, a trillion-dollar market[35] that leans heavily on women. In Eve Rodsky's book, *Fair Play*, she recounts a conversation with University of Southern California psychology professor Darby Saxbe, who researches the gendered division of labor. "The wellness industry is certainly hip to imbalanced gender roles," Saxbe said. "Women need to ask themselves—what's more transformative to my life? A new serum for dark circles or *a more fair and balanced division of labor in my home?*"[36]

Rodsky laments, "Hopefully one day, Fair Play [a system for how to divide up household tasks fairly, based on your needs][37] will be a three-player game that includes meaningful state and federal policies. In the meantime, and in this country, Fair Play is a two-player game that requires change to happen from within your own home."[38] And if you're a single mother, then yes, this is reduced to a one-person game. All the more reason we need state and federal policies to help alleviate the burden you face single-handedly.

FINDING BALANCE

For women drowning in the mental load of motherhood, there are things we can do to balance the responsibilities with our partners without extensive couples therapy (although I would never dismiss therapy if it's an option), long, drawn-out fights, or calling the divorce lawyer. I've already mentioned some books completely devoted to the subject (and they're listed under *Lighten Your Load* below), but Rodsky's book *Fair Play* offers a few tips.

RECOGNIZE VISIBLE VERSUS INVISIBLE WORK

Rodsky looks to the redistribution of home labor as a way to have an open, constructive dialogue with your partner on how to understand what's at stake and the roles each of you plays. Rodsky argues that "visibility equals value," and recommends mapping out what each person currently does to help point out all the visible and invisible work we do to keep the household running. If this sounds daunting, Rodsky has done the work for you, and you can find the tasks on her website fairplaylife.com/the-cards.

…THEN REDISTRIBUTE IT

Mapping out who does what in a relationship and then shifting toward a more equitable distribution requires—gulp—a conversation. I know, I know, but sadly, until someone invents a device for mind reading, our partners don't know what they don't know. And if they don't know there's a problem, how can they help with a resolution? When the *Huffington Post* asked divorced women what they could have done differently in their marriages,

"I wish I would have asked for help when I needed it" was a common response.[39]

ALL TIME IS EQUAL

It is crucial that both parties recognize that all time is considered equal, whether one partner is working for a salary or home doing housework or if both work but one person's salary is higher. Work is work. One kind is not more valuable than the other. Your time matters because you matter. And not just as a mother but as a person.

GIVE EACH OTHER TIME TO DO WHAT YOU LOVE

Both partners can and should make space to engage in something that drives their passion. You don't need your partner's permission to do it. So many mothers lose their identity in motherhood. It's easy to get swept up in the role and to let go of things that used to bring you joy. I remember feeling so guilty for going to the gym for just an hour the first time after having Kevin. But why? My time to do things I love (yes, I love to work out) is just as important as my spouse's weekly soccer games. As humans, as partners, and yes—as parents—we owe it to ourselves to take the time we need to fill our tanks. As a society, we have no right to criticize or judge a parent who still follows their pre-parenting dream and pursuits. We should applaud them.

Once you and your partner have reviewed your tasks, decided how to redistribute, and crafted a more level playing field, then you each can own and execute your responsibilities in the most efficient way. No more nagging, eye rolls, or deep-seated contempt. The result? More mental space for you.

In many ways, the hopelessness that Gemma and I felt during the pandemic remains. It's easy to feel dismay at the stats, the unsupportive narratives, and even the systemic regression. Look no further than the overturning of *Roe vs. Wade* in 2022 to make us feel like we are going backward in the women's movement.

But do you know who else lacks support? Dads. Men's involvement in parenting responsibilities is stifled by lack of resources, outdated systems, and even cultural bias. Consider the continued lack of changing stations in men's restrooms. Another example? Men receive significantly less paternity leave time than women; only 5 percent of new dads take two or more weeks after the baby is born.[40] Dads also have much less access to community support than mothers. A survey by Massachusetts General Hospital showed one-third of expecting fathers do not believe they have support or information about fathering skills.[41]

If we are going to move mothers forward, we need to support and advocate for fathers too. The stigma of fathers who put their family first remains abrasive, and we need a massive cultural shift to reset the playing field so it matters less if your title is mom or dad and to offer tools and resources for the only title that should matter: *parent.*

Rome wasn't built in a day. In fact, Rome had to crumble a few times before its glorious resurrection. I want to believe we are in the groundbreaking awakening of a new outlook on parenthood and parenting structures. If change starts in the home, then perhaps a reset of gender roles in today's modern household are the building blocks that will completely reshape what it means to be a mom and dad in this country. Otherwise, we will simply crumble yet again.

LIGHTEN YOUR LOAD

- Have a conversation with your partner about your mental load; discuss their mental load as well. Write down each of your responsibilities and discuss where you can reasonably shift some weight over to your partner.

- Seek outside help if you can: babysitters, a cleaning person/service, a meal prep or grocery delivery service. We live in an incredible time where we don't ever have to walk into a grocery store again (thank you Instacart!). I also save a ton of money by outsourcing my trips to Costco because I don't impulse buy. If your budget allows, see if there are expenses you can cut to make room for a service that would significantly ease your burden. Or consider in-kind services.

- There are books devoted to this subject that should be required reading for every couple with a baby. *Fed Up* is an introduction to emotional labor. *Fair Play* offers specific tips to better shift the workload in a relationship. And the aptly titled *How Not to Hate Your Husband After Kids* by Jancee Dunn offers more real-world advice with some humor laced throughout.

- Rethink who does what in your household. Just because you're home with the children does not automatically make you the dinner cooker and laundry folder. Nor does your partner get stuck with unclogging toilets and helping with homework just because that's how it's always been. Step away from how your parents did things, too, and talk realistically about which chores are responsibilities you want to have, do well, or what makes the most sense. We sometimes go on autopilot in our home roles because it's what we know from growing up. Let's shake things up!

- "I recommend that after the birth of a child, both individuals in a couple commit to giving their partner a three-hour window once a week," said Shane Kelley, PhD, a psychologist based in Reno, Nevada, who specializes in couples. "For example, every Saturday from 9-12, a dad/partner takes baby and the mom/partner gets to do whatever she wants with no judgment about her choice (either from herself or her partner). The point of this is to have a time during the week when no one needs to ask for a favor and no one needs to feel guilty about whatever it is they feel like doing for their 'window.'" Kelley suggests using the time to do whatever feels most relaxing and recharging, such as sleep, reading, exercising, self-care, or time with friends.

- Several movements advocate for working mothers and the unique challenges we face, such as the American Families Plan, a government plan designed to improve tax cuts for working families and at long last guarantee twelve weeks or more of paid parental leave across the nation, and the Marshall Plan for Moms, a national movement to create change and advocate for mothers, as well as policies around equal pay, parental leave, and programs to retrain mothers who left the workforce for extended periods of time to raise children.[42] Moms Rising is a grassroots organization working to achieve economic security for all moms, working toward paid family leave, affordable childcare, and ending the wage and hiring discrimination against mothers. Follow these programs on social media or subscribe to their email newsletters to learn ways to build awareness and spark change.

♦ Here's a variety of responses from my social media followers after asking what they do to ease the mental load of motherhood every day. Helen said, "I exercise hard. Aggressive training reduces my anger about other areas of my life." Gretchen says, "Therapy, cycle classes, and *lots* of books about recovery and sobriety." Colette: "I started to learn how to share it with my husband and he has stepped up!" And Jennifer probably says it best: "One friggin' day at a time!"

4 | HOW'S MOM REALLY DOING?

MARIE'S* STORY

"I was a really high-functioning drinker," says Marie, thirty-nine. "I very much had it all together on the outside. Three kids, good career, married for eighteen years. And I worked really hard to make sure it appeared that way. But on the inside, it was so much different. I had huge issues with self-esteem, depression, and anxiety."

The image of alcohol was ingrained in Marie's life from her earliest years. She describes family party pictures of her and her cousins as young as two years old "cheers"-ing with milk and water in shot glasses. It was a huge part of her family dynamic, and it was understood early on that this is just what people do—they drink.

Even when her father struggled with his own alcohol addiction and ultimately began attending AA, it was all very hush-hush. Marie recalls hearing her father talk often about attending meetings, but it never registered that those meetings weren't for work.

Marie started drinking at fourteen and she always went big. "I didn't have an off button. I wanted to take it too far every

---

*Name changed for privacy

time," she tells me. When she met her future husband in college, they connected as both big partiers and heavy weekend drinkers.

But while her husband would abstain from drinking on the weekdays, Marie couldn't cut herself off, even though she felt hard pressed to do the same. Soon she found herself drinking in secret to avoid her husband's judgment, even though they both drank hard on the weekends together.

When she became a mother, her desire to drink only grew. "Mommy Wine Culture was exactly the excuse I needed to continue my problematic drinking without raising suspicion," said Marie. She now realizes she is deeply introverted, and that alcohol helped her open up and make friends with other moms.

Marie's drinking came in starts and stops. She'd take breaks from drinking but always picked it up again. "I felt like I was broken. I thought I knew what an alcoholic looks like, which was my dad who had three DUIs, and I've never had any of that. So if I'm not an alcoholic, what am I, and what is wrong with me? I thought I was the only person in the entire world who couldn't figure this out."

Her husband became increasingly suspicious of her problem as Marie started embarrassing herself at family gatherings, picking fights with him, and losing control more often. He confronted her, and she agreed she needed to work on drinking less. She started reading sobriety books and listening to sobriety podcasts. She would take breaks but inevitably convince herself she could do it better this time—only to fall harder and faster.

Things came to a head after one afternoon at a family gathering. Marie's dad, almost seventeen years in recovery at this time, handed her a shot. She took it and tipped it back without a second thought, even as her daughter sat next to her and her husband looked on in disbelief. She could see his eyes screaming, "What are you thinking? Your daughter's watching you and it's four in the afternoon!" She knew her drinking had gotten out of control, and she saw the implications it was having on her family, yet she couldn't stop herself from slipping back down the rabbit hole as that one shot turned into another blackout. Marie walked a metaphorical tightrope between the expectations she and her family had around alcohol and her desire to be a good mom and stop disappointing her loved ones over and over. And she'd just slipped off again.

The next morning she took her kids to a trampoline park with a raging hangover and had the epiphany that she was tired of her own self-sabotage. She vowed, yet again, to quit drinking alcohol that day, but this time it stuck. She was ready to make peace with the idea of an alcohol-free life, and she's now three years sober.

"I'm trying to change the narrative for my children. We talk about everything; no question is off limits. And I think that if I took anything from my childhood, the silver lining is my kids are going to grow up knowing that [alcohol] is a part of our family history. I wonder if someone had talked to me then, maybe I would I have made different choices? I didn't get the full picture, and I really want my kids to have the full picture."

SOFIA'S STORY

There's a specific memory Sofia, thirty-four, has of applying for WIC (a nutrition program for low-income pregnant and postpartum women and children) as a single mom desperately trying to make ends meet. And getting denied for having too high a salary from her job as a teacher to qualify.

Sofia remembers thinking, "I'm a single mom. I'm trying my best and I'm barely surviving. I was so upset that they had denied me cheese and bread and basic shit that I needed."

Sofia drove herself and her one-month-old baby to a bar, crying. "I remember telling the bartender, 'Look, I just need a dark place to sit by myself, where nobody's going to judge me,' and he was like, 'Don't worry, nobody's going to judge you here.'" Sophia remembers drinking at that bar with her one-month-old in the car seat at the foot of her barstool.

Sofia felt alone, suffering, thinking there was no safe place to go. She also says that as a Latina, she felt that her culture didn't encourage her to admit she needed help or was struggling, that asking for medication and mental health support can sometimes feel taboo or be misunderstood—even bring shame to the family.

Sofia's story is not uncommon. How many women experience severe postpartum anxiety and depression but feel too ashamed to seek out help or even know help is available?

Sofia met someone new, and they got married. After her second child was born, she again suffered from PPD and remembers having suicidal thoughts. "I wish that I would have gotten on medication a lot sooner, but I didn't. I felt like people who take medication were weak or couldn't handle it, whereas now I'm on medications for anxiety and depression."

Sofia also lives with an autoimmune disorder, and heavy drinking combined with the various medications she was taking for that condition made her prone to blacking out. Still, her drinking got progressively worse, and in 2021, she almost died of alcohol poisoning.

With her husband's support, Sofia came home from the hospital grateful to be alive and determined to quit drinking. "I felt like that was a real turning point. I definitely feel like God was in the middle of that [night] because even in the ambulance, the EMT? Her name was Grace."

Excerpt from a post I wrote and originally published on Scary Mommy October 31, 2016, two years before I quit drinking:

Do you self-medicate? I do.

After a long day at home or a stressful day at work, I definitely feel like I earned that glass of wine at dinner. Sometimes when I've gone a few nights with little sleep, I'll pop a Tylenol PM to move things along. Is this terrible? Am I well on the path to AA?

I read an enlightening article in The Atlantic[1] about how moms self-medicating with booze has become so common and so ingrained in our society that we don't even realize how unhealthy a habit it is and what it inevitably leads to. The article says that in the '70s and '80s, pop culture promoted pill popping more than booze. But since they discovered that pills like Vicodin are ridiculously addictive and dangerous, society has moved to the ever-present wino momma.

The article delves deeper into why we need to self-medicate in the first place. The pressure we are putting on ourselves to be all things is so overbearing, so unsustainable, that we need that release just to survive. I believe it. Some days, I'm so wound up by the end of the day, I get nauseous to the point where I think I'll throw up. Other days, I'll get headaches the size of boulders crushing my skull.

Last night, I lost my mind at exactly 7:18 p.m., just as I was giving my son a bath and getting him ready for bed. I felt myself physically shut down. When my husband saw the look on my face, he promptly took over bedtime duties and told me to go lie down. He's seen that look before. It's not pretty.

What's a mom to do? Last night, I went to bed at 7:30 p.m. because I could. But I can't do that every night. Normally night-time is prime time for getting the kids' lunches ready for school the next day, washing the dinner dishes, moving the clothes from the washer to dryer so they aren't all mildewy by morning, and paying bills—because even after my mommy duties end each night, my responsibilities as an adult remain.

But as if moms don't feel guilty enough, now we need to feel guilty about this luxury too. I understand the reasons, but I still feel myself scream inside, "No, people! Don't take this from us too!"

I cannot deny that I let that guilt chip away at me. Addiction is a strong force in my family history. I remind myself that with every sip. Can I still enjoy this pleasure while that truth tugs at me? Am I playing with fire every time I pop open a cork?

And if I do put the wine glass down, do I need to find a different, healthier way to self-medicate? Perhaps. Or do I need to find a less stressful way of living all together? Kick the root cause out the door. But seriously, I don't know how realistic that is. In this world where parents are superhuman caretakers, breadwinners, Pinterest fiends, and PTA members, we are expected to do it all while sporting six-pack abs. No excuses—unless you want to be "that" mom, the mom who other people whisper about, who can't get her act together, doesn't seem that engaged in her children's passions, or never seems to have her priorities in order. Now that's a stigma I never want to have.[2]

Abstaining for forty weeks during pregnancy makes it easier for moms who may have questioned their relationships with alcohol to convince themselves that they really don't have a problem. Many women I've talked to in the recovery community speak to a similar feeling. They say, "Pregnancy was all the proof I needed that I could stop whenever I wanted. See? I'm in full control, but hand me some alcohol now because nine and a half months was long enough."

At the time I didn't connect my interest in alcohol with providing a way to numb any issues I was having in my life. I partially believed that the beauty and gift of parenthood would somehow fix or heal my deeper struggles. That this new meaning—it's called the miracle of life, isn't it?—would resolve or at least mitigate my internal struggles and lead to an understanding of what really matters. Perhaps I'd finally grow to recognize just how much I matter, too.

Pregnancy and childbirth do not fix us. Motherhood does not heal trauma. And raising a newborn does not change our intrinsic mental health challenges, meaning someone with anxiety and depression will still deal with those same issues down the road.

I know that probably sounds obvious. But a part of me believed that my new identity as a mother would resolve some of my deeper anxieties and concerns around spirituality, living a life of purpose, perhaps even help me to understand where I fit in the plan that God and the universe had for me.

Life certainly had other plans for me, and PPD came in like an avalanche in those first weeks. In fact, my anxiety only got worse, and I began having intrusive thoughts of all the ways a baby can die, whether I was around him or not. When I was holding him, I worried he wasn't breathing or that I would drop him. I feared he would get sick. Did his color seem off? And when I wasn't holding him, new visions emerged of him choking, suffocating, or succumbing to SIDS. I used to joke that I spent half my days trying to quiet the baby and the other half wondering why the baby was so quiet. Only I wasn't casually wondering; I was sick with anxiety, checking him constantly and never able to relax.

I felt like a fraud. I was trying desperately to convey confidence and self-satisfaction in this role as a new mother, a role many of us dream of since childhood. But nothing felt further from the truth. I was drowning in self-doubt, terror, and regret. And people around me made it worse. "Enjoy these precious moments," they would coo in the checkout line at the grocery or in line at the post office. The words would sting my open wound. Enjoy? I was literally living second to second. I wanted this moment to be over. I wanted to fast-forward to a time where my baby was self-sufficient, healthy, and strong. Where I could look at him with relief knowing he was going to be OK. I would tell myself that things would be easier when he could hold up his head . . . start to crawl . . . begin eating solids . . . The fear followed me like a shadow, never satisfied with the present moment.

My feelings of anxiety morphed so naturally to guilt. I don't deserve this. I don't deserve him. My sweet, beautiful baby who I don't know how to care for properly. Anyone could do this better. Someone should do this instead of me. While so many moms are heartbroken to say goodbye to maternity leave, I welcomed returning to work. I was sure that the day care teachers were far more qualified to care for my baby than I was. I was flying by the seat of my pants and convinced that everyone knew it.

Looking back, I want to shake my fragmented spirit and infuse some strength into her. I'd tell her, you are worthy! You are deserving! You can do this! This is your baby, and you are capable. There is no one more qualified to raise this little human than you. You will be scared. You will be tested. You will cry and scream and feel more emotion in a day than you've felt your whole life. But you are good. You are just right. You are enough.

The fact is, it wouldn't have mattered. I now know that negative voice was PPD and anxiety speaking. I needed medication. I needed support. What did I not need? Wine.

MOMMY DOESN'T NEED WINE

It seemed so very easy to lean on a little alcohol each night. No need to involve others. My struggles can be my little secret, and no one would bat an eyelash at a mom sipping a glass of wine after the baby goes to bed.

My doctor prescribed an antidepressant and made no mention that alcohol would counteract many of its benefits. I didn't bother to ask, although a simple review of the prescription label would have clued me in. It never even occurred to me that my glass of wine might not only be hindering my PPD recovery but actually making it worse.[3] It angers me to think about this now. Every day was like climbing Mount Everest just to make it to bedtime, and I felt certain something in me was broken. I knew it wasn't supposed to feel that way, I just didn't know what else to do.

After I stopped breastfeeding, I remember the feeling of liberation, like I finally had my body back to myself. I could take over-the-counter medication without having to scroll kellymom. com (a breastfeeding database) up and down for which remedies are considered safe in breast milk. Of course, it also meant that I could be less inhibited in my alcohol consumption.

When we took a big family trip to Mexico right after the transition, I loved having margaritas by the pool and wine aplenty. I felt like after everything my body had been through—pregnancy, giving birth and breastfeeding, now raising a tiny human—I truly deserved to let loose a little. My mom and in-laws were more than happy to have baby time while I enjoyed some day drinking on the beach.

My "letting loose" time didn't last long, as we were blessed to hear the exciting news that I was pregnant again later that year with Ben. This pregnancy flew by, because Kevin was practically galloping by this point and never sat still.

My ability to drop my wine habit so easily convinced me I had nothing to worry about. I must not have my father's genetic predisposition toward alcohol dependence.

When Ben was born, it was a very different parenting experience. Ben had a very mellow, easy demeanor, and coming off our experience with Kevin's colic and acid reflux, we were relieved. This felt manageable. This felt doable. I would put Ben in his bassinet, and he would (gasp!) fall asleep. Gone were the hours of bouncing and cooing and wiping my own tears while I tried to remember what the baby books advised if steps one through four didn't work.

I thought this time I would be better prepared for PPD, if it did emerge, but those first few months I felt good—euphoric even. Maybe I wasn't such a terrible mother after all.

But PPD did come for me, when I least expected it. I was six months postpartum, and I didn't know I was still susceptible. One in seven women struggle with postpartum depression, and it can present itself at any time in the year after childbirth.[4] In a meta-analysis of eighty-four studies on the links between PPD and risk factors, researcher Cheryl Beck cited ten factors that make someone more likely to experience it. Referred to as the Postpartum Depression Predictors Inventory, the list includes:

- ◆ Prenatal depression—This may be the strongest predictor for later suffering from PPD.

- ◆ Prenatal anxiety.

- ◆ History of previous depression—Although not as strong a predictor as a depressive episode during the pregnancy, it appears that women with histories of depression previous to conception are also at a higher risk of PPD than those without.

- ◆ Maternity blues—Especially when severe, the blues may mark the onset of PPD.

- ◆ Recent stressful life events.

- ◆ Inadequate social supports.

- ◆ Poor marital relationship—One of the most consistent findings is that among women who report marital dissatisfaction and/or inadequate social supports, postpartum depressive illness is more common.

- ◆ Low self-esteem.

- ◆ Childcare stress.

- ◆ Difficult infant temperament.

Beck's same inventory acknowledged an additional three factors that consistently arise to increase a woman's risk of PPD, especially in combination with one or more of the factors listed above:

♦ Single marital status.

♦ Unplanned or unwanted pregnancy.

♦ Lower socioeconomic status.[5]

When I look at this list now, in hindsight, I clearly see myself in it. Previous history of depression? Check. Low self-esteem? Duh. Prenatal anxiety? How about 24/7/365?

But when I look deeper, I feel the knot in my stomach tighten. Childcare stress, inadequate social supports . . . I see the mental load of motherhood factoring into several of these indicators. I wonder how many women fall into postpartum depression—or more recent labels of postpartum rage and anxiety—fueled primarily by the mental load mothers carry. And I see the socioeconomic factors and heavy barriers single mothers already face contributing to their likelihood to experience PPD on top of everything else.

Anyone who has experienced depression knows it's a very dark time. Depression can completely zap your energy, even the will to live. When you incorporate a baby into the mix, depression takes on an entirely new level of terror, guilt, or perhaps most perplexing, apathy. We find coping strategies that can look unusual or even alarming to those around us. Maybe we start working more or simply can't get out of bed. We might feel disconnected from our baby. Sometimes we develop unhealthy coping patterns around feelings of fear or anger or deep sadness. Ultimately, it comes down to trying to deal with internal suffering, and in all of us that will look different.

Less known but no less common is postpartum anxiety, all-consuming fear and worry after having a baby. Postpartum anxiety affects up to 21 percent of mothers and often goes undiagnosed since health care providers do not currently use a screening tool to diagnose this condition.[6] Most commonly, it is identified during a PPD assessment by the provider, as they often occur together. At this time, researchers do not know a lot about postpartum anxiety, and it hasn't been studied as much as PPD. As we learn more, I hope we can identify and diagnose it sooner so new mothers can get the support they need.

The Substance Abuse and Mental Health Services Administration (SAMHSA) here in the United States reports that approximately 15 percent of women who identified having PPD engaged in binge drinking, compared with women who did not give birth or who did not mark having PPD.[7]

It saddens me now that our society encourages women who are susceptible to depression, rage, anxiety, and hormonal fluctuations in general to drink—perhaps even preys on women who are such an easy target through Mommy Wine Culture.

The lack of attention and focus on postnatal maternal health is especially ironic given the amount of doctor visits facilitated and encouraged in the health care system following a child's birth. In a 2009 study on the effect of alcohol intervention on postpartum depression, the study states, "Unfortunately, although new mothers typically have increased contact with primary health care providers (including obstetricians and gynecologists, pediatricians, nurses, and internists or family practitioners), oftentimes mental health issues are not disclosed."[8]

Why? Well, for one thing, doctors rarely ask about the emotional or psychological state of the mother. Generally, these appointments are focused only on assessing the health of the baby and the physical healing of the mother. In an interview with NPR, nurse-midwife Karen Sheffield-Abdullah says, "We are so baby focused. Once the baby is here, it's almost like the mother is discarded. Like a Reese's Peanut Butter Cup. The mom is the wrapper, and the baby is the candy. Once you remove the wrapper, you just discard the wrapper. And what we really need to be thinking about is . . . that time after the baby is born."[9]

Unfortunately, as I experienced, the stigma and shame a new mother experiences if she doesn't feel grateful and blissful can far outweigh any desire to call attention to such misgivings. In fact, new moms may even be worried that it's a risky proposition to reveal those feelings, for fear they might alarm a medical professional. I remember a powerful feeling of self-disgust because, even though my prayers had been answered by birthing a healthy baby, instead of feeling grateful I felt sad, scared, and inadequate. How could I express that to the medical professional who helped me deliver the baby or played an integral role in my prenatal care? Sometimes it seems easier to simply keep quiet and hope the feelings pass. Or more often? Find other ways to cope.

Women are good at keeping quiet when it comes to our own mental health. According to the American Psychological Association, 20 percent of mothers refrain from opening up about possible symptoms of a postpartum mood disorder.[10] In an article for NPR, Dr. Alexandra Sacks, a psychiatrist specializing in maternal mental health and reproductive psychiatry, says, "Many women falsely believe that admitting they're anxious or depressed is the same as admitting weakness. They may even fear that speaking about their feelings may make them more real. We need to do a better job explaining to patients that anxiety and depression have nothing to do with being a 'bad mom.'"[11]

It takes shame up another level. And so we see mothers dealing with anxiety and depression who begin to self-medicate with alcohol or drugs. While the data on new mothers who misuse substances is limited, I'm certain that the numbers we do have are vast underestimates, since so many women either use substances secretly or cloak it in what appears to be ordinary social behavior.

"The co-occurrence of mental health issues and substance use disorders is very common," Dr. Indra Cidambi—the medical director and founder of the Center for Network Therapy—said in an article for Scary Mommy. "In fact, suffering from a mental health issue as a teen or adolescent increases the chances of substance abuse later in life. Almost 50% of people who suffer from mental health issues also suffer from substance use disorders—and vice versa. However, it's important to note that while there is a strong connection between substance abuse and mental health issues, substance use usually does not lead to mental health issues. Rather, it is a symptom of a pre-existing condition."[12]

We are in a mental health epidemic, there's no question. The World Health Organization (WHO) reports a 25 percent increase in anxiety and depression within the first year of the COVID-19 pandemic, citing women as more severely impacted than men. In addition, gaps in health care services only made the situation worse.[13]

WHAT MOTHERS REALLY NEED

So what's a mom to do? And if one more person tells me "self-care" is the answer, I'm going to flip a table. But seriously, we need to offer mothers more than just the Instagram-post definition of self-care as bubble baths and massages. And what about the huge number of us who are actively raising kids as primary caretakers? *"Excuse me, sweet baby and toddler, while I go take a weekend girls trip to relax . . . "* Yeah, it doesn't always work like that.

Tessa Stuckey, a licensed professional counselor, parenting coach, and author of *For the Sake of Our Youth*, offered suggestions on realistic things mothers can do when they are feeling especially anxious. Stuckey suggests really deep breaths, which signals the nervous system to relax. She also suggests taking a self-imposed time out. "I think taking little timeouts can be really helpful. It is okay to say mom needs a couple of minutes. It lets our kids know that we are human as well. If that means connecting with a friend who you can just vent to, text them and say, 'Is now a good time for me to call you because I really need to like process some of this stuff.'"

Women get a bad rap. We can't express anger or frustration or suffering sometimes without serious backlash or criticism. If we express any negative emotion, we get called bitch or bossy or a nag. People say, "It must be that time of the month" or we are called emotional or dramatic. So many of us hide our emotions. We bury them inside and let them eat us alive. No wonder we are struggling.

If you're angry because you're the only person in the family who picks up clothes off the floor, allow yourself to feel angry. If you are overwhelmed and feeling burned out because you are doing three jobs for the price of one? Get mad. Use that energy for something constructive. "Anger is a catalyst," says Brené Brown. "It's an emotion that we need to transform into something lifegiving: courage, love, change, compassion, justice."[14]

No one gets a medal for being the best at internalizing their feelings. Moms don't get rewarded for staying quiet when we are dying inside, for going about our days like we aren't screaming silently. What if all of us spoke out or demanded change? What a forceful fire we could spark together.

My grandma always said, "The squeaky wheel gets the grease," and I think when it comes to our mental health and doing what's needed to take care of ourselves, we could all use some grease right now.

LIGHTEN YOUR LOAD

- New mothers who feel symptoms of a mood disorder, including anxiety or depression, can and should talk to their doctor. If that is not an option, the organization Postpartum Support International is a resource that offers mom-to-mom contact with trained volunteers.

- If you do not have an OB that feels supportive and focused on your mental health pre- and postnatal, find a new OB if at all possible. If it's not an option, advocate for yourself or bring a loved one to your appointments with you who can help convey your symptoms and support you.

- Dr. Anna Lembke suggests a practice of "radical honesty" as a way to make better decisions. "We can wake up in the morning and say, 'Today, I'm going to try to go through the whole day and not tell a single lie about anything. And if I do, I'm going to try to correct it as soon as I possibly can, even if it seems small and inconsequential.'" It sounds minor but making these small daily choices helps us manage future planning, delayed gratification, and our overall mental health.[15]

♦ "Women need real moments of solitude and self-reflection to balance out how much of ourselves we give away."— Barbara De Angelis.[16] Begin journaling or start an affirmations practice as a means of self-care and reflection. Journaling and affirmations are backed by science as a way to affect our brain with positive neurochemicals that boost physical and emotional health.[17] *The Self-Love Workbook for Women* by Megan Logan, MSW, LCSW is one I use, but there are plenty to choose from.

♦ There's a hilarious TikTok trend that shows someone aggressively walking to peppy music with the text overlay: "Me going for a stupid walk for my stupid mental health." It's funny because it's true. Physical activity, whether we like it or not, improves our physical and mental health. Better still? "Exercise improves mental health by reducing anxiety, depression, and negative mood and by improving self-esteem and cognitive function."[18] So, go for a stupid walk. Your mental health will thank you!

5 | THE HERD MENTALITY

ANNA'S STORY

"I'll never forget one work trip in London," Anna, thirty-nine, reminisces. "It was 11 p.m. And people were clearly getting kind of tipsy."

Anna had quit drinking after realizing that she had a toxic relationship with alcohol, but the tech company she worked for had a heavy drinking culture. One night after hours together with her colleagues, "I told them it was time for me to leave and a senior director there said, 'No, you can't leave. The only reason we all get together is so we can all get drunk together.'"

Being the sober person in a drinking culture can be challenging at best, and downright miserable and triggering at worst. Scariest of all? Your job may be at risk if you try to establish boundaries. Instead of being rewarded for doing something healthy, you get labeled as someone who's "not a team player."

"I don't think a week goes by where I don't encounter multiple jokes about needing a glass of wine or that it's five o'clock somewhere. It puts you in this really awkward position of having to smile and nod—which is often what I do—but it demeans who I am a little bit. The alternative would be to tell them I don't drink and that's awkward too, plus people have questions about why. It's something that makes me feel kind of 'other' pretty frequently."

No one should feel pressured to drink, at work or outside of it. Anna now is working with the HR team at her company to create a more inclusive workplace around this issue and others. While she has several years of sobriety under her belt, someone at her company who might be in a more vulnerable place may appreciate a safe space or camaraderie at work. And with time and dialogue, we can reach a place where being sober in any industry or workspace is no longer the equivalent of a scarlet letter.

From my blog: July 24, 2021

I think one of the greatest disservices of our times is the notion that a person either has a drinking problem or doesn't.

For most people, a drinking problem does not flick on like a light switch. It is a slow accumulation of years of a growing toler-ance in addition to life circumstances.

I spent years doing mental gymnastics over whether I was in control of my drinking. I believed I was. But during those years, my tolerance grew and grew until I could consume a bottle of wine without feeling drunk. Combine that with an environment where moms are encouraged to drink to cope. And a social narrative that if you haven't lost everything due to heavy drinking, you're prob-ably fine.

Mixed with my generalized anxiety and depressive episodes, alcohol, the marketing around it, and the social narrative supporting it all played a part in my belief that alcohol made things better, when in reality it made me feel a thousand times worse.

I remember telling this to someone shortly before I quit drinking. I told him the headaches, the foggy brain, and the energy drain were just too much.

Maybe I needed to stop drinking altogether.

The man, in all seriousness, nodded in understanding before suggesting I lace my coffee with some hair of the dog. And if that isn't the perfect example of how our alcohol-heavy culture assures us that we need to drink more, not less—then I don't know what to say.

It's often a slow burn over years for us to realize the house is, in fact, on fire. Maybe it's time to stop asking if we have a drinking problem and start asking if drinking is causing a problem.

In other words, don't wait for the house to burn down, but listen for the smoke alarms. And if the alarms go off? You don't ignore the smoke and go back to bed. You get the heck out of the house.

Oscar-winning actor Anne Hathaway made headlines when she announced on the *Ellen Show* that she was quitting drinking for the next eighteen years while her son is living in her house. "I don't totally love the way I do it," she grimaced.

It was a powerful statement coming from a household name, and an important reminder of the effects alcohol can have on parenting, even for the rich and famous. I personally felt validated by Anne's statements, as I'd had a similar epiphany that I, too, could not be a drinker and the parent I wanted to be simultaneously.

The world had something to say, as it always does, about Anne's decision, and not everyone was supportive. Zoe Williams wrote a tongue-in-cheek article in the British newspaper *The Guardian* that was less than positive, titled, "Anne Hathaway is giving up booze for 18 years to be a better mother? I can't drink to that." The piece states "[Anne] doesn't want to do nursery drop-offs hungover, which will make it difficult for her to make friends, but she is American and they do things differently there."[1]

When a Facebook friend of mine posted about the piece, multiple people mulled over whether or not this was a serious article or "British humor." While the group ultimately agreed it was intended to be a joke, it seemed like a sinister one, complete with damning judgment and condescension. Williams writes, "Parenting, including drunk parenting, is a tremendous bond, a leveler, a source of shared amusement; you fail, you try again, you fail better. . . . I was reading my son a book the other day in which someone drinks themselves to death. . . . He asked me: 'Can you die from too much alcohol?' I said: 'Sure, but you'd have to drink a hell of a lot.' And he replied, 'How come you're still alive?'"

"God. This is more proof of what I told my best friend last week," Sandy Black[2] commented, on the article. "I never felt the peer pressure to drink in high school that I feel now. It is even worse in the UK. Abstaining is like some kind of alien concept. Say it and you get poured a glass anyway because you can't possibly be serious."

Another woman bemoaned, "It amazes me that at forty years old I still find myself feeling the need to explain myself as a nondrinker."

The pressure to drink? It's real, and it's dangerous.

And if you're a mom? It's almost expected.

When I think of herd mentality—the phenomenon when people conform their views and behaviors to fit into a group—I think of cults, TikTok trends, and seemingly everything in high school. Social media especially plays to the herd mentality because it empowers seemingly random things online to go viral. Remember the ice bucket challenge from way back? Raise your hand if you participated in this challenge or know someone who did. Similarly, the corn song blanketed social media in the summer of 2022, and seemingly everyone wanted to participate in this catchy song about corn. Was it because everyone is passionate about corn? Maybe, but more likely it's because folks are more inclined to share something all their friends are sharing or what they think they'll be sharing.

Herd mentality is inextricably connected to social media because social media algorithms are designed to show us more of what we want to see. We scroll through our feeds and see how friends, influencers, even celebrities portray motherhood. We see them doing everything we seem to struggle with. We read posts that glorify motherhood and remind us we only get eighteen summers. We see social media influencers curating picture-perfect scenes of raising babies and toddlers without a tantrum or mess to be seen.

And when we do struggle? When we speak up and say "I'm not OK," does our proverbial village—made up of our own friends and family, mind you—finally come out to save us, support us, or lift us up? No. Instead, we get judged, shamed, and called bad moms. We are told to go to the psych ward. We are considered needy, incapable, or asleep at the wheel. Our village tells us we are doing it wrong.

Beth Berry states, "It's not simply overwhelming that parenting standards have risen dramatically while support systems have vanished, it's an unfair setup that has mothers thinking their personal inadequacies are to blame for what is actually the fault of a broken system and distortions of reality."[3]

WHEN MEMES DON'T HELP

I write a lot online about parenting, and I have a wonderful, loyal Facebook following of mostly women. While the majority of my readers are at various stages in raising their kids, my page is geared primarily toward new-ish moms. When I was frustrated with the daily wine memes that bombarded us, I posted a meme about not needing wine to be a parent. In fact, that wine (for me) makes things harder.

It reads: "The house is a mess, the kids are screaming, my partner is grumpy and I need to make dinner. Friend: Sounds like you need wine! Me. No. Wine is actually the opposite of what I need."

When I posted this, I knew I was heading into murky territory. Social media is a place to broadcast your love for wine. Talking about how wine can be harmful? Not so popular.

I was impressed, though, with the particularly large number of people who liked, commented, and shared the post. "Love this! So true! Alcohol does not help. It makes me less able to think and respond to the crumbling situation around me" was one comment. Another woman wrote, "Yes, yes, and yes. It's so sad that in today's society we feel the need to encourage moms to drink. You should not need alcohol to cope with life."

But then came the negative responses. Some women got downright defensive.

"Let's not demonize a glass of wine now. Oh lawd, people always have to make a point of everything like moms that have a glass of wine and relax are drunks," one responder commented. Another woman wrote, "We don't need running shoes to run, but it helps."

I was stepping outside my comfort zone. Suddenly my Facebook page's following, which had grown steadily through my writings on motherhood, mental health, and female empowerment, was evoking unexpected controversy. The responses got nastier. More than aggravated, some people responded with outright rage. I started getting comments like "c*nt," "snowflake," and "another Karen." Just yesterday someone commented, "LOL addict." I've always been conflict averse, so at first it was terrifying and made me wonder if it was worth going head-to-head with popular opinion.

Margaret Heffernan, bestselling author and entrepreneur, wisely puts it this way: "We know—intellectually—that confronting an issue is the only way to resolve it. But any resolution will disrupt the status quo. Given the choice between conflict and change on the one hand, and inertia on the other, the ostrich position can seem very attractive."[4]

I admit, the ostrich approach had its allure. I considered ignoring this problematic messaging that seemed to be everywhere. I could step back and focus on the blessings of motherhood. No one could argue with that, right? But the more common the memes linking moms and drinking were, the more I started to think about why, how, and at whose expense those offhanded comments were being made.

Making jokes that allude to addiction or coping with alcohol is a message of privilege that can and does get weaponized against minorities. "Wine mom culture lets white women cosplay as 'bad moms' because they're given the benefit of the doubt that BIPOC moms aren't afforded," says Tomi Akitunde, the founder of mater mea, a content platform for Black mothers, in an interview for *Wine Enthusiast Magazine*.[5] Vena Moore's article for Medium, "Wine Mom Culture Excludes Black Mothers," expands on this. "Black mothers don't have the luxury to joke openly about imbibing. Many of us can't even think to put memes on social media about wine being our equivalent to a man's toolbelt." Vena goes on to say, "Does this mean that Black mothers don't drink? Of course not. But due to the oppressive double standards they live under, they may be more likely to downplay their drinking."[6]

Why are people so completely invested in this mommy wine narrative? Why does the topic stir up so much passion in people? Why does a person pointing out the darker side of this 'Mommy Wine Culture' generate so much fear? Naïvely, I wanted my story to connect with all moms, not just those struggling with their drinking. Instead, I saw the subject create a tremendous divide: women who understood and took it seriously and women who saw my message as a threat.

Is this just a wine meme joke that went too far? Have we really reached the point where we need wine to help us through our daily tasks the way runners need running shoes? Or is this yet another contrived message that continues to keep women down?

Regardless of why my writing became such a trigger, the effects of these memes, and the T-shirts and the mugs and the health studies that warp facts into a catchy headline can be devastating. They were to me, at least.

Where some might have seen just a funny wine meme, I saw justification to drink. Where some might have seen a brief, breezy read about the benefits of wine, I found validation for what was becoming an increasingly troubling habit for me.

When I was drinking, I would share these wine memes to build my wine-drinking mom squad. Let's laugh and praise the glory of our destructive wine habits together, people, and it won't feel so dangerous.

Everyone likes Buzzy Betty, the happy-go-lucky mom in the Facebook group that shares funny memes and pokes fun at needing to fill her thermos with booze to make it through the PTA meeting. Am I right? Do you know who no one likes? The Sober Sally who kills every buzz with the inevitable: "Here's what's wrong with this message."

And yes, both Betty and Sally were me. Going from "Never a bad time to wine" to "Not on my watch!" Over time I stopped expressing anger and frustration with the *what* and started to dig deeper into the *why*. Why have we turned to humor instead of exploring the pain we're feeling and finding solutions to it? Instead of spending time sharing wine memes, what if we wrote letters to our state legislators or our company's HR department demanding better maternity leave options? If we took a dollar from every "mommy needs wine" purchase and instead invested in affordable mental health resources for moms struggling . . . can you imagine the impact?

Every so often, I will speak up if I see a wine mom meme that is particularly harmful or when celebrities use the wine mom trope for an easy like or sell. To me, all this is more than just stupid wine sayings on a shirt or a mug. Behind every Buzzy Betty lies another overwhelmed mom doing the best she can with the tools available to her. It's not her fault she is validating her behavior with self-effacing humor; it's the system she's navigating that seems so determined to break her down. Don't shoot the messenger—call out the system instead. But also? Enough with the mommy wine jokes.

In *Wine Enthusiast Magazine*, of all places, an article titled "Meme Girls: The Wine Mom Phenomenon Speaks Volumes"[7] dug into the history of wine marketing to women and the evolution of the wine mom phenomenon. Author Rachel Tepper Paley acknowledges "the meme continues to evolve—and may soon represent something entirely different." The concept of a wine mom may be broadening to include anyone who is overwhelmed, overworked, and not taking care of themselves properly—parent or otherwise.

Along with a transformation in mindset, perhaps the drug of choice is shifting as well. Cannabis mom, anyone? This might be the most frequent question I'm asked: What are your thoughts on cannabis mom culture (although it's often posed more like "Mommy needs a joint though, right?")? Here are my thoughts on cannabis moms: same problem, different drug. Like Mommy Wine Culture, it's not really about the substance. Whether it's mommy's little helper, wine, or marijuana, it's all speaking to the same problem—mommy's struggling and we are turning our backs on her in a time of need.

Sometimes I'll get asked, "Well, what about coffee?" Coffee mom culture is even more prevalent than wine moms. Caffeine is considered a drug too. But, and it's a big *but* here, coffee has never led to a parent losing custody of their children. That being said, coffee sure seems to be a preferred tool for parents who are overwhelmed and underserved; parents who need to be all things to all people regardless of whether they got enough sleep the night before. On the other hand, coffee isn't mind-altering and has never led to a DUI, so let's give coffee moms a break on this one.

Finally, let's speak to beer dads for a minute. I know the question is coming: How can I talk about Mommy Wine Culture and not speak to the pressure dads face to drink beer or whiskey or other types of hard alcohol? Men face a unique challenge related to the intense pressure to drink, especially socially or around sporting events. The market research shows that Big Alcohol pushed hard to connect drinking at sporting events in order to attract a male audience (at one point Anheuser-Busch was sponsoring twenty-three out of twenty-four Major League Baseball teams).[8]

But mothers are already overburdened in the day-to-day household responsibilities, so targeting moms particularly feels extra unsettling. When you consider stats around the increase in drinking in the past thirty years, women constitute a significant portion of that increase—and at an alarming rate. "For nearly a century, women have been closing the gender gap in alcohol consumption, binge-drinking and alcohol use disorder," according to Kaiser Health News. "What was previously a 3-1 ratio for risky drinking habits in men versus women is closer to 1-to-1 globally, a 2016 analysis of several studies suggested. For people over 26, women are increasing their alcohol consumption faster than men."[9]

Clearly more factors are at play in the increase in women's drinking than just Big Alcohol's push to win us over, or we would see likewise increased consumption statistics in men. But with the additional responsibilities women generally carry and the societal expectations for women to just "handle it" (nod to Olivia Pope in the TV show *Scandal,* who clutched her glass of wine while outsmarting the most powerful men in DC) without complaining or seeking support? Voila. We've got millions of women self-medicating with the most easily accessible and acceptable drug on earth.

TOXIC DRINKING CULTURE

"It's not alcoholism until you graduate" a common saying goes in college circles.[10] College binge drinking is pervasive in the United States, with 80 percent of college students consuming alcohol and 50 percent of those students reportedly engaging in binge drinking. In fact, 31 percent of college students meet criteria for a diagnosis of alcohol abuse.[11]

In college, herd mentality drives what many of us now consider a normal part of the college experience. Students drink to fit in, to socialize, and to party. And while the ramifications to all students who drink are clear—physical and mental health risks, academic problems, and addiction[12]—women are especially prone to potential physical or sexual assault when alcohol is involved. And let's be clear: how much someone drank is irrelevant when it comes to blame. Full stop. Assault is no more or less justified when the victim is blackout drunk or stone-cold sober. According to Rape, Abuse & Incest National Network (RAINN), 13 percent of undergraduate and graduate students experience rape or sexual assault, and about three-quarters of those students identify as female.[13] The reason women are far more susceptible is an indictment of the broader toxic patriarchal system, not of the women themselves.

Yet even with the increased risks for women, especially when they're impaired by alcohol, college drinking is often when our toxic relationship to alcohol takes hold. Even now I look back on my own college experience and remember equating college to a hall pass for drinking. Films like *Animal House* and *Old School,* which glorify college drinking life, validated this.

Perhaps this would be a different conversation if we all settled into healthy drinking patterns after college, but that was not my experience, nor is it for so many. So is going to college a likely precursor for alcohol addiction? While it's certainly not that simple and I've found conflicting data around that question, alcohol. org does state that, "binge drinking at a young age, including college, is linked to an increased risk of developing an alcohol use disorder (AUD)."[14] And it's been shown that college students have higher binge-drinking rates than their noncollege peers.[15]

If you are feeling your heart sink as you think about what this means for your kids, I offer some hope. Research shows that students who opt out of drinking often tie their decision to conversations with their parents about alcohol use and consequences.[16] Talking to adolescents about the data around alcohol use on campus will help kids recognize that while it may feel like everyone drinks, that is not the case. Offer suggestions around how to decline a drink in front of friends, talk candidly about your own drinking experience in college, and remind them of the ways alcohol affects the body and impairs function, logic, and clear consent.

While binge drinking might have been a large part of the college experience in years past, with continued education and dinner table conversations with our kids, we can help shape a new college experience for future generations.

Drinking culture looms especially large over women in the workplace environment. Workplace drinking culture has always been a thing (martini lunch, remember?), but with more women in the workforce, many can feel pressured or encouraged to drink to keep up with "the boys" in order to have a "seat at the table." While it can be safe to have a drink after work, an environment with heavy drinking during or after work not only increases physical risks, mental health consequences, and possible addiction—it puts us at far greater risk for sexual harassment and/or assault.

But what's the alternative for someone who doesn't want to drink at all? Decline drinks, seek out nonalcoholic alternatives, or opt out altogether. These choices can also have consequences. I remember overhearing an old boss once say about a job candidate, "Well, she said she doesn't drink. I can't imagine someone working here that doesn't even drink."

The small start-up I worked at for over ten years was steeped in casual drinking. Afternoon parties in the manufacturing side of the building were complete with alcohol, cigars, even pony kegs on occasion. One of the few women at the company, I took regular trips to Europe with male colleagues for trade shows, where drinking started at lunch and nights would be capped at ten or eleven o'clock after a full day of drinking with customers. Indeed, drinking was a part of the experience, and I sometimes wonder if my willingness to imbibe as well as my high tolerance were reasons my male colleagues liked having me along on these trips.

"The social stakes of workplace drinking cultures can be forebodingly high, especially for individuals who choose not to drink," according to an article in *Access Health News*. "Avoiding company events centered around alcohol is a risky decision, as it may result in social isolation or jeopardizing working relationships. . . . The unspoken and often confusing protocol around workplace drinking creates enormous social pressure to conform and consume alcohol, whether or not employees feel comfortable with such substance use."[17]

Women have been working hard to climb the corporate ladder for decades, and mothers know the ramifications of feeling left out of events, judged, and overlooked for promotions already, simply by virtue of being a mom. While I didn't quit drinking until a year before I left the start-up, once I had my first child, I was never asked to travel for a trade show again. To also decline evening drinks out or social events that revolve around alcohol only further alienates us from the group.

After I quit drinking, I became increasingly uncomfortable during drinking-focused events at work. At the same time, I didn't see the point in sticking around and watching coworkers act silly or joke around—sometimes at my expense. While I never openly spoke to my coworkers about my sobriety, it can be hard to hide it in certain settings, and it made me an easy target as the only woman in an all-male, heavy drinking environment. I left the company shortly after I was one year sober.

MAKING A CHANGE

How do we effect a change in messaging and dismantle the targeting of mothers specifically? Basically, how do we stop making the women's struggle the butt of the joke? If herd mentality is the cause of much of this narrative, I think herd mentality can also be part of the solution. There are several opportunities to enact positive change, some specifically around Mommy Wine Culture and others geared around mental health.

We need to speak up about the dangerous undertones of Mommy Wine Culture. Education is key in helping people understand the root cause of this narrative. Speaking to the dangers of alcohol in general will help, as will the increasing number of women coming forward to speak up about their decisions to quit drinking (regardless of their reasons). Celebrities like Adele and Jessica Simpson are coming forward to discuss openly the positive impact their sobriety has made on their lives, and they are helping to normalize sober living.

A social media acquaintance of mine, Anne Bodenstine of @mom.whine.repeat, has a popular Instagram account with more than 110,000 followers. Her original handle was @mom .wine.repeat before she changed it, and I reached out to Anne to learn more about this change. She said when she first was coming up with the name, "@mom.wine.repeat seemed catchy and simple, representing two things that were a big part of my life at the time, being a mom and drinking wine."

She didn't give it much thought until a few years later when a reporter for *the Atlantic* reached out to interview her for a story. Exploring the popularity of Wine Mom Culture and equating the "wine mom" identity "to mean something similar to 'Karen': a wealthy white woman who, well-meaning as she may be, is blind to her own privilege." The piece concludes that perhaps instead of wine what moms really need is better support.[18]

Anne said the article "made my heart sink and an uneasy feeling grow in my stomach as I realized that this was not what I wanted or intended to portray with my Instagram account. I was kind of embarrassed that my name was associated with this article and wished that I hadn't done the interview." She began to question her own relationship with alcohol, especially when a paragraph from Holly Whitaker's book, *Quit Like a Woman*, hit a little too close to home: "The ace up Big Alcohol's sleeve is a woman with an Instagram account."[19] "I knew right then that I needed to change my Instagram handle, and coincidentally this was around the same time that I myself stopped drinking alcohol," said Anne. "It was no longer serving me and I knew that I didn't want to represent the Mommy Wine Culture in any way whatsoever." It's changes like these that can steer the conversation in the right direction, and I hope it's a trend we continue to see rise.

We must continue to demand a more equitable distribution of labor at home, in addition to more flexibility in the workforce. The increase in parents working from home since the COVID-19 pandemic has made a difference for many, adding a flexibility factor we never saw while working in full-time office environments.

I've made a firm decision to work only for a company that embodies a deep understanding and respect for parents who need to drop everything for a phone call from school or a sick kiddo. I can make such a choice thanks to both the privilege I enjoy as a middle-class white woman and twenty years of work experience that have made me highly sought after in my field. I'm hugely grateful that I can have such flexibility, and I don't take it for granted. I recognize I'm in a place many are not, which is all the more reason we should collectively strive for this in the entire modern workforce. The goal: a work life where employers encourage their employees to manage their own work-life balance, knowing that a contented and healthy work force contributes to an environment that's best for everyone.

We should work to end the stigma around mental illness, including depression. We can do this by sharing our stories. We can reshape our children's future, where stigmas and shame no longer dwell in the shadows. By showing our friends and family there is more to us than picture-perfect Instagram feeds and filters. Also, speaking openly about anxiety, depression, addiction, and recovery, we can reshape what it even means to be normal. Imagine how connected we could become if we broke through the superficial BS of niceties and told people how we are really doing. I believe we would save lives. At the very least, we would shift perceptions. This is bigger than normalizing therapy, antidepressants, or mental illness. This is about celebrating our unique selves with and through our struggles.

We must start treating Big Alcohol more like Big Tobacco by holding the alcohol industry accountable, pressuring them to communicate the health risks of their products. Look, it's a lofty goal, but we were able to do it for the tobacco industry, so dream big with me here. I'd also like to see more emphasis on education and additional research to further understand the dangers of alcohol. But I think minimizing the marketing of alcohol in media and including health warning labels is spot on. Also, selfishly, I would love to be able to get through a single show or movie on Netflix without the protagonist clutching a glass of wine or whiskey neat like their life depended on it.

We must connect and communicate with teens, preteens, and even kids in elementary school on the risks of drinking and the effect of alcohol on the body. Jessica Lahey wrote an entire book on preventative measures to reduce the risk of addiction in our children. In *The Addiction Inoculation,*

Jessica reminds us, "genetics matter, but they are not destiny," and "genetics are about 60 percent of the picture and the rest comes down to environmental factors."[20] What's more, "Children who grow up with addicted parents are 'primed' genetically, emotionally, and experientially for addiction."[21] *Gulp.*

So what's a parent to do? Obviously, this is a very nuanced topic, and the kind of conversations you have with your children depends on their ages, but the key is communication. Lahey states that children as young as three can identify and differentiate alcoholic beverages, so if you think your child is too young to start talking about it, think again.[22] Consider, for example, the TV shows, movies, or YouTube videos our kids are watching. I felt sick watching the animated film *Arctic Dogs* with my five- and three-year-olds when a scene that strongly alluded to the main character (a cute little arctic fox) getting blackout drunk the night before. He was gagging like he was going to puke and had sharpie marker all over his face. When he looked at pictures from the night before, he was clearly horrified that he had no recollection of those moments. My point is, unless you're living under a rock, your kids are likely being exposed to alcohol culture much sooner than many of us would like to think. Creating an environment where they feel comfortable asking questions or sharing concerns is crucial to opening these lines of conversation.

We must demand workplaces make efforts to eliminate toxic workplace drinking culture. When Google discovered that in 20 percent of their sexual harassment cases the perpetrator had been drinking, they changed their policies around alcohol at work and work-related events, forbidding excessive drinking at work or during any business-related event. They also held managers responsible for discouraging heavy drinking.[23]

"Given how much time most of us spend at work (and how stressful that environment can be) it's not surprising workmates loom large in shaping drinking behavior," Flip Prior says in an article for ABC Everyday.[24] When we spend eight or more hours a day with some people who include alcohol in virtually every activity, it can heavily influence our habits or drive unhealthy drinking patterns. But opting out of five-o'clock drinks every Thursday with your colleagues labels you as "not a team player," regardless of your reasons. Which is why we need to set firmer boundaries that drinking and the work environment are better off separated. But old habits die hard, and drinking at holiday parties, networking events, and trade shows are all considered par for the course. If we cannot prevent overlap altogether, we at least need to offer nonalcoholic options and alternatives (other than water) so nondrinkers don't feel like social pariahs or worse—start drinking again because they fall prey to overwhelming peer pressure.

The status quo is changing rapidly, and when it comes to reshaping harmful narratives, that is a good thing! If sharing our stories is an impactful way to help end stigmas around addiction and mental health, then herd mentality might be our dark horse to help us reshape some of these narratives.

Maybe all it takes for us to reverse toxic messages, dangerous drinking conditioning in places like college or the workplace, and the presumption that mommy needs wine to get through parenting is making space for new messages. Raising awareness of our truths. Flipping the script on the more damaging narratives around alcohol by using the same platforms, trends, and strategies that got us here to begin with. Because people are tired of unrealistic, toxic, disenchanting messages. We want real, honest, and relatable. Let's give people what they want.

LIGHTEN YOUR LOAD

♦ Curate your social media to follow pages and people who inspire you and lift you up. Unfollow ones that don't. Also, if certain things or people online trigger you—to drink, binge eat, or just feel bad about yourself, you know what to do. Even better, if you see alcohol ads on Facebook, you can click on the top right to avoid seeing ads like these. You can even narrow it down to say no more ads about alcohol at all. *Boom!*

♦ Curate your IRL friends too. You don't have to say goodbye to your drinking buddies forever, but it might be wise to stay away until you have solid sober footing. Skip the wine walks and the beer fests for a night in with Netflix. Again, not forever. Give yourself permission to opt out of people's lives who don't push you to be better. Yes, we are talking boundaries here. I saw a meme that said, "The people in your circle should be rooting for you. If not, get a new circle." Spend your time with people who genuinely want to see you succeed in your sober journey.

♦ Come prepared to parties, dinners, even PTA meetings. Always have a nonalcoholic drink in hand. It's an easy way to say, "No, thanks! I've already got one," if someone asks if you'd like a drink. Whether or not you want people to know you've quit drinking or are taking a break, it's nobody's business until you want it to be. This is a great way to avoid the question altogether.

- Remember, everything is not about you: the wine memes, the fitness instructor saying "You've earned a glass of wine" after a tough class. You just don't need to hear it, right? People aren't trying to piss you off, they're just living their lives. Which is also why your lecture about how drinking alcohol even moderately increases a woman's chances of breast cancer by 15 percent[25] might be better expressed at a different time and place. Remember, it's *your* journey.

- Find out what your state legislates for maternity leave; every state is different. Contact your local legislators and advocate for at least three months paid maternal leave for all new mothers. Fight for paternity leave for new fathers. Better yet, get the men in the family to do it. Redistribution of labor can start here.

- If you work in an environment that fosters a toxic consumption of alcohol, offer to help coordinate upcoming events that aren't centered around booze or suggest to the event committee that they include nonalcoholic options.

- Anna, whose story is included at the beginning of this chapter, took matters into her own hands by suggesting to her company's HR department that they initiate a community group centered on sobriety. Many workplaces are focused on company diversity, equity, and inclusion. An employee resource group centered on sobriety is a valid ask and a great opportunity not only to educate your colleagues and the HR team but to offer a safe space for other employees who need it.

♦   I asked my social media followers for input on how they deal with peer pressure to drink. Lauren said she limits "my circle exclusively to people who don't suck," which I love—we could all take note here. Colette says, "I seek out activities that don't involve alcohol." Luisa said, "Now I can say I just don't want to drink, but I used to invent excuses all the time." Julie: "I've been sober for seventeen years. I'm proud and talk about it all the time."

6 | WHEN THE FUN STOPS

KRISTI'S STORY

When it comes to the downward spiral, Kristi, thirty-eight, fell hard and fast. While she always assumed she would drink less when she started having children, the mental load of motherhood exacerbated by traumatic birth experiences (one child who spent the first month in the NICU and another with a cleft lip and palate) left her feeling overwhelmed and undersupported.

While her husband returned to work full time, Kristi was left to carry the load of early parenthood, raising three small kids.

As resentment in her relationship over her husband's hands-off approach continued to build and all the stressors of raising kids increased, Kristi turned to alcohol to numb out the feelings. "I felt helpless, powerless, angry, and very alone. I think I drank away how hard that all was."

Kristi enrolled in an eating disorder outpatient program to appease her husband and family, even though she knew deep down her real problem was alcohol. A few days later, she wound up in a psych ward after sneaking in alcohol and blacking out. Her husband told her she could not return home until she went to rehab, so she went but was still unconvinced she had a problem. After her fourth child was born, her drinking really skyrocketed.

Her husband served her with divorce papers, and Kristi finally realized if she didn't quit drinking, she was going to lose her kids. She went to a new rehab and stayed for two months. "It was the first time I ever probably showed up for myself. This time at rehab felt completely different—it was the first time I ever considered staying sober for myself."

Kristi is almost three years sober and happily single. She prioritizes her sobriety and her children, and she is being more vocal about sharing her story publicly in hopes of inspiring other women.

Blog post from December 25, 2020

It is not even 6 AM and as I scroll through social media on this Christmas morning, I already see a post showing a tray full of mimosas.

I know that for many, drinking on holidays is just a given. But if you are someone who is questioning their relationship with alcohol, I ask you this . . . after that first mimosa, or after that sophisticated glass of wine that makes you feel tall and fancy, what comes next?

Do you sit in satisfaction, grateful for another year? Or did it trigger a preoccupation over where you'll get your next drink?

Do you find yourself in a mental space where you can't even sit in appreciation or gratitude because you've flipped the switch and now your body demands more?

If that second scenario is where you're headed, I only suggest you ask yourself if it's worth it.

Is it worth the next several hours trying to chase the buzz?

Is it worth the questionable things you might say or do as your body shifts into autopilot while your family and children watch in despair?

This is for you to decide.

I'm just here to remind you to consider how the day will play out after the first drink.

I know how easy it is to get lost in the romance of the first drink.

But unless you're someone who can stop there, the fantasy of satisfaction dies fast. And what you're left with is a slow descent into the dark.

It's a darkness I don't ever want to feel again. And it's a darkness, as the daughter of an alcoholic, I don't ever want my children to witness firsthand.

So I will stay sober this Christmas. Because I know where that first drink leads. And I know that for me, it never stopped at one.

I've lived in Reno, Nevada, for almost twenty years. The city is often considered a smaller-scale Vegas, thanks to its dozen casinos, video poker at many bars, and even slots lining the airport's halls.

Anywhere you go in Nevada with a slot machine, poker table, or a sports book, a small stack of brochures can be found nearby. For as long as I can remember, the brochure cover shows a sunset and says in big letters: "When the Fun Stops."

The brochure is from the Nevada Council on Problem Gambling, and it directs folks to a hotline for problem gamblers. By law, these small pamphlets are required anywhere gaming is available in the state.

When I was younger, child free, and used to spend more time on a barstool, I would pick up one of these pamphlets every now and then to amuse myself while killing some time or use it as scrap paper to write something down. I remember thinking just how sad the brochure looked and felt. I couldn't imagine how miserable and hopeless a person had to get to reach for this dusty, worn brochure and read through the different signs of a gambling problem, a quote or two on the pain of losing everything to gambling, and the subsequent number to call for help. It seemed to me, that by the time someone was calling a problem gambling hotline, the fun must have stopped quite a long time before.

If I could remake that pamphlet, I would give it a different title. I would say something like: "When you are sick and tired of your own BS," or "When you can hardly look at yourself in the mirror anymore." Sure, they're not gambling specific, but I think they're far more in touch with the place in life someone might be to seek out these resources.

Dr. Lembke says that when we repeatedly expose ourselves to any pleasure-producing stimuli, our brains end up needing more and more of those stimuli. When we are using our drug of choice, whether it be alcohol, sex, or compulsive gambling, then it "doesn't even get us high. It just makes us feel normal. And when we're not using, we're experiencing the universal symptoms of withdrawal from any addictive substance, which are anxiety, irritability, insomnia, dysphoria (feeling generally dissatisfied) and craving."[1]

So habitual drinking goes from fun and rewarding to simply feeling normal. And in the hours we abstain? Well, that feels like boring, exhausting, slow going—about as much fun as watching paint dry.

CHANGING THE NARRATIVE OF SOBRIETY

When I think about the final years of my drinking, it's clear that the fun had stopped long before I was ready to get serious about change. The only thing that kept me hanging on was the fear of what a life without alcohol would look like. Without drinking, could I ever have fun or experience pleasure again?

And can you blame me? In our society, we portray sobriety as miserable. People in recovery are failures. Outcasts destined to a life of weak coffee and basement meetings. Movies and TV offer us the token sober character who is just one poor choice away from a relapse.

This is how I used to visualize sobriety. Boring, miserable, sad. Sobriety was the last stop at the train station before the train went off the tracks. It meant failure, deprivation, and disease. Is it any wonder, then, how many of us are hesitant to seek support or help? I am reminded daily why I kept my sobriety a secret for a full year before telling anyone besides my husband and mother. Because when you say "sober," or "drinking problem," or "alcoholic," the crowd stiffens a bit. Some label me as no fun, a buzz kill. More recently, I get called a "Karen," which I believe speaks volumes about how unpopular sobriety can be.

I would love to see this narrative change. I would love to see society embrace the sober lifestyle. When the term "sober curious" started gaining traction a few years ago, it felt like we were heading in the right direction. Dry January and Sober October—monthlong commitments to going dry—started to trend. But then the pandemic hit and it felt like hashtags supporting dry living transitioned to #quarantinis and #drinkingathome. For every two steps forward, it seems we go two steps back.

Where are the sober-empowered badass women I found through my recovery and adore in real life? Why aren't more of the women in media portraying strong females and showcasing sobriety as a feminist manifesto for symbolically refusing to numb away our power?

When someone quits drinking, people want to know what made them quit, but nobody ever asks someone why they still drink. People assume the worst when someone stops drinking—that they'd hit rock bottom. They'd lost everything. They'd been ordered into treatment by the courts. And instead of celebrating or congratulating the person for making the best choice for their own health and life, people question their decision, worse yet, try to pressure them to have "just one." Just this last weekend, I attended a group dinner and when both the person next to me and I asked for water, an acquaintance laughed and said, "party poopers." This was a group of people in their thirties, forties, and fifties, mind you!

If you want to know what a real party pooper looked like though, you would have to time warp back to me in the last year before I quit drinking. I was starting to black out more frequently. I was more focused on my drinking than what anyone else was doing or talking about. I would need a full day to recover from a binge, chugging Gatorade and popping Advil and Pepto every few hours, and I was having zero fun. None. Nada.

It didn't happen overnight. I suppose that's why addiction is so damned tricky. Alcohol dependency is progressive, and it can take years to reach the tolerance level and develop the inner justification for drinking a bottle of wine a night because "I don't even feel drunk yet."

Lines that only a few years ago we'd never dream of crossing eventually get crossed, and then some. Kristi said it so well: "I had never woken up in vomit on the kitchen floor, put champagne in my coffee cup, or gotten a DUI . . . until I did."

And we're not alone, as stats continue to show a significant rise of drinking, especially in young mothers. But even so, not everyone is waking up in vomit and not everyone is tossing back a bottle a night . . . a lot of people are reading this who may be "gray-area drinking" or simply sober curious. Or maybe the fun hasn't stopped yet. Maybe you feel safe because you don't have a family history or you only drink "clean wine" or you've read that wine is heart healthy. Should you still be wary?

Quite simply, yes.

THE DANGERS OF ALCOHOL

What's Wrong with Using Alcohol Anyway?

Someone commented on my Facebook page the other day, "I use alcohol to cope. So what?" It's a fair question. After all, for decades alcohol has been pushed on us as healthy, safe, fun, sexy. . . . It's legal, it's *everywhere*, and 80 percent of the population drinks, so really—what's the harm?

I want to preface this section by saying there are a lot of books completely devoted to this topic. *This Naked Mind* and *Alcohol Lied to Me* both dive into the science around what alcohol physically does to our body, as well as the mixed messages we receive through the media on alcohol being heart healthy, safe in moderation, and even beneficial for socializing, enjoying sex, or relaxing—all of which these books adamantly debunk. If you want to really drill down on how alcohol affects your brain, your heart, your liver, your immune system, and yes, your sex drive—run, don't walk, to the nearest bookstore or library and pick up one of these books ASAP.

I'm just going to focus on a few key points to help connect the dots between women, mental health, the mental load of motherhood, and the dark web of interconnectedness alcohol has to them all.

Alcohol is a depressant, which means that drinking any amount will negatively impact your mental health. "The evidence has increasingly shown that there is no level of alcohol consumption that is safe for health," said Beatriz Champagne, chair of the Advocacy Committee at the World Heart Federation.[2] Knowing this now, I'm fascinated to constantly hear people say they are having a drink because they had a bad day or, perhaps more perplexing, because they are having a good day. Why would you want to consume a depressant in either situation? I think about how often we celebrate momentous occasions—weddings, baby showers, anniversaries—with a mind-numbing depressant. It's wildly counterintuitive, and yet it's just how it's always been done.

The other factor to remember here is the link between alcohol misuse and depression. While we covered mental health in chapter four, I would be remiss not to add here that women are more than twice as likely to misuse alcohol if they have a history of depression.[3]

So if people with depression are more likely to engage in substance misuse, and women with depression are more susceptible to substance misuse than men, women with PPD who choose to drink put themselves in a precarious position. It would be one thing if it helped in any way, of course, but it doesn't. It makes things markedly worse.

I am convinced that parenting hungover is our very own self-imposed hell on earth. It's not as simple as nursing a hangover while rocking a baby back to sleep, although TV or movies sometimes make it look that way. In how many TV shows have I seen a parent sleeping off last night's antics and wonder to myself "Did the writers forget the character had children at home?" Kids don't sleep in on days when mom or dad's nursing a hangover. I swear, kids feel our pain and exhaustion and they feed off it. Kevin's colic amplified my "hangxiety" (hangover anxiety) and made me irritable and exhausted. With my second son, Ben, simply navigating two kids at the same time made my head ache more. Add the screaming, fighting, and constant pulls and tugs for attention, and it was a recipe for misery.

So if drinking was causing more problems than it was solving, maybe it was time to start looking at other options.

The "sober curious" movement, a phrase coined by author Ruby Warrington and described in her book by that name, started to build in 2018.[4] The concept is to give up alcohol, not because of struggles with addiction but because of the health benefits from going alcohol free or for other personal reasons. Some of the recommendations from Warrington's book include not drinking daily and never drinking more than anyone else at a party. I cringe at how damned obvious her suggestions seem as I read them now. Things like "[making] sure you aren't hurting those around you."[5]

I look back on my own drinking history and want to scream in frustration because the problem now seems so obvious. It's like when you're watching a horror movie and know the murderer is upstairs but the woman goes up the stairs anyway. *Don't go up the stairs, lady!* But when you're in the middle of it, it's not obvious at all; you don't even register the trouble your drinking is causing. That's why Warrington's book was so important. It normalized not choosing to drink, it encouraged curiosity around sober living, or even simply dedicating yourself to a Dry January. No big deal. No judgment.

Before the sober curious movement, it was assumed that if you opted out of drinking, it would be for religious or health reasons. I never considered <u>if</u> I would go back to drinking post-pregnancy, just <u>when</u>. It was absurd to think that I'd abstain from alcohol if I was anything less than an alcoholic, like my father. I'd felt confident in proving time and again that I had control over my drinking and therefore wasn't damned with the family curse of addiction.

After my PPD with Ben, I felt my drinking take a darker turn. I needed more alcohol than just a glass each night, but I didn't want to stir up suspicion or concern, so I got sneaky about it. I started drinking out of coffee mugs. I would sneak pours when John wasn't looking. I wasn't getting plastered every night, but I was clearly getting more uncomfortable with my own actions.

When a box of wine would empty, I would wrap it in a plastic bag and throw it out at a gas station or grocery store trash bin and buy a new one to replace it before anyone noticed its empty space in the fridge. I would cover beer or wine bottles with miscellaneous recycling to hide the ample evidence from anyone who might be keeping an eye on our trash cans. John. The neighbors. The trash collectors. No one could know how much I was really drinking, and the fear of being exposed or getting called out kept me constantly on edge and feeling guilty.

I see the irony of it all now. I grew up with a father whose family secret was hiding his liquor, and here I was, doing the exact same thing. But at the time I had a thousand ways to deflect. *I don't have a problem. I don't drink before 5:00 p.m. Look, I do well at a good job. I can go days without drinking. We are not the same people, my father and I, and his mistakes should not define me, or stop me from having a fulfilling life.*

Except it wasn't fulfilling. Nothing about trying to maintain my excessive drinking and keep it a secret was fulfilling. My secret alcohol habit only took and took from me. It left me paranoid and always one mistake away from getting caught. I would wake up in the morning after a binge and check my phone to piece together what I'd done the night before. Did I call anyone? Text? Post on social media? Is my husband talking to me or does he seem angry? I would spin a web of possibilities in my head about what did and did not happen and what kind of damage control I'd need to activate. Most nights, it was minimal. Some nights I really messed up.

Catherine Gray, author of *The Unexpected Joy of Being Sober,* refers to these little and big moments as "Convincers." Convincers count as anything that "added fuel to my desire to get sober. . . . They're pitch-black moments in my life, but they serve a bright purpose in the long-term. It's because of those blood-chilling moments that I finally scraped together the wherewithal to start swimming as fast as I could for the sober shore."[6]

When psychologists review a patient's diagnostic criteria for alcohol use disorder, they encapsulate two concepts: problems tied to drinking and loss of control. Psychologist Shane Kelley says, "Problems are not just DUIs or losing a job. Problems can be arguments with your spouse, parenting in a way that is not optimal, or trying to focus on health and physical fitness and alcohol use interfering with those goals. Loss of control can be subtle as well—waking up and wishing you had less to drink the night before is indicative of some level of loss of control."

My Convincers and signs of losing control were growing bigger and coming quicker. They included the day at the church, and the words from the pediatrician. They were a regrettable tweet, or a fight with John I could barely recall. Nights not remembering when I went to bed, or waking up with no clothes on. Every moment added fuel to the fire, and the fire was growing bigger and brighter.

I was sabotaging my health, my family, my marriage, my very existence. I was risking it all with my drinking habit that was spiraling from uncomfortable to deeply disturbing. And for what? For a short-lived buzz. The fun had stopped. In its place sat a house of cards carefully holding itself together through shame, fear, and deceit, and ready to topple at any moment.

LIGHTEN YOUR LOAD

♦ Write a pros and cons list of the ways alcohol serves you and how it doesn't. How much on your list is based on what you think will happen versus how you actually feel? Include a column for the science and health effects of each entry, and add your Convincer moments to your list. How does your alcohol consumption affect your family? Your work? A lot of articles suggest writing a list of reasons to quit, which is great, but it's also important to see what your reasons are to keep drinking and look at how much of the "pros" are heavily influenced by marketing messaging, myths, and the influence of implicit bias. Implicit bias means automatic and unintentional bias for or against something, and it can affect our subconscious decisions and behaviors. Many of us experience implicit bias around alcohol based on how our parents drank, the news, and social media.

♦ A lot of people resort to completing an online quiz to determine if they are drinking excessively. There is no accurate quiz to determine if you have a drinking problem, unless the quiz asks how alcohol makes you feel: when the fun stops, you have the answer to your question. Trust your gut, get curious, seek out resources. Quit-lit and self-help books are profoundly enlightening in helping us understand what drives us. I steered away from consuming media around problematic drinking for fear of it hitting too close to home. I think subconsciously I was afraid of what I would learn or see, and I wanted to wade in my pool of blissful ignorance for as long as possible. What I now know is that hiding from the truth may have delayed my decision to quit, but it also delayed my opportunity to find the inner peace that only comes with overcoming addictive behaviors and/or substances. Ignorance may mask as bliss at the time, but it comes at a steep price to your health, relationships, and quality of life.

♦ Talk about your drinking concerns with someone you love and trust and get their honest feedback. If this prospect leaves you shaking in your boots, tell a counselor or a spiritual advisor. My local church connected me with a counselor who listened to my concerns and helped me process my feelings. She also recommended a "Life Changes" small group at the church that I found healing and connected with others in. If that's not an option, try saying it out loud to yourself or writing it down. Often when we speak out loud or write down our feelings, we can see something more clearly than when we let our heads control the narrative.

♦ Take a break from alcohol. Try going one month dry. Dry January gained popularity as a one-month alcohol-free challenge; in 2022, 35 percent of legal-aged Americans participated.[7] But if you missed it this year, have no fear: Dry July and Sober October are also increasingly popular options. If you want to try but would like some coaching or inspiration along the way, Annie Grace has a great thirty-day challenge called the Alcohol Experiment with an app that includes lots of helpful info. The more uncomfortable you feel at the idea of going dry for a set number of days, the more important and productive this dry month will be. Sometimes our greatest growth comes from doing things that make us uncomfortable.

7 | STARTING THE SOBER JOURNEY

COURTNEY'S STORY

"Everything they tell you not to do in the first year of sobriety? I think I did most of it," laughs Courtney, age thirty-seven, as we talk about her sober journey. Courtney tells me she is coming up on four years sober, and she finds tremendous solace in her recovery path despite her many transitions that first year. During the year in which we spoke, she'd reconciled with her husband after a near divorce, the family moved, both she and her son experienced major health scares and surgeries, and she lost touch with her AA home group.

As a military spouse, Courtney and her family are familiar with the regular relocations that come with that job, but they always left her feeling very isolated and lonely. The challenges of parenting alone while her partner was deployed for months at a time led her to alcohol.

"I thought to myself, 'I'm awake, I'm alive, I'm the best mom ever,' and I would travel to the park with my Yeti full of alcohol. And [my kids] had no idea that I was sitting there sipping on alcohol while they're playing at the park. I thought it was OK. This is how we, as moms these days in this generation, this time, this is how we have to cope with parenting. This was normal. This was fine."

Courtney's kids were three and six when she quit drinking, but Courtney mourns the pain she caused them at such young ages. "I'll never get that time back with them. And that's probably the saddest part about it. I can make new memories now, which is great. But it affected them more than they'll ever know: Mom's always in bed. Mom's always hungover, or constantly yelling at us for no reason."

It took her husband handing her divorce papers to wake up to the reality of her situation. She was going to lose everything if she didn't quit drinking. And even then, it was years of relapses and slips before it finally clicked. "AA saved my life," Courtney affirms. She committed herself to the process and now she reaps the rewards of long-term recovery.

LAINEY'S STORY

You don't have to hit rock bottom to stop drinking.

Lainey, age thirty-five, had probably heard that expression plenty of times before, but for some reason on that day listening to those words from a sober podcast really sunk in.

"For me, it just clicked, and I got this sense of peace that washed over me. I started to think about all the fun things I could actually do and remember clearly if I was sober."

Lainey shifted her perspective from what she would lose in sobriety to what she would gain. She thought about time and activities with her kids and never having to worry about driving drunk.

She joined a recovery group for moms, Sober Mom Squad, and started attending online meetings. She remembers hearing one story in particular from another mom that resonated deeply.

"She said exactly what I was feeling—being so sick of feeling her feelings." Lainey realized her fears weren't around alcohol but about feeling everything—good and bad.

By understanding her "why"—the reason she drank—the real work of healing could begin. Lainey met with her doctor and started on an antidepressant, which made a huge difference for her anxiety. "It worked so well for me," she beamed. "My life totally changed by ninety days [sober]." And Lainey credits community for helping her make connections with other mothers in the same boat as her.

Lainey is now a meeting host and still an active part of her sober community. She says when she hears other moms say they feel like they need a drink, she thinks, "No, you know what you need? You need a nap. And a hot shower. You need someone to make you a casserole and do your laundry."

When I talked to Lainey for our interview, she had just celebrated seven hundred days sober.

Blog post from September 15, 2021

I still remember an urban legend I heard in my 20's about someone's dog.

It was my boyfriend's old roommate's friend's dog, or something. It was just one of those stories that gets passed down and you don't really know how much of it's true. But anyway, the guy left his dog at home for the weekend and gave him enough kibble to last the few days he would be gone. But apparently dogs don't understand how to ration and the dog ate all the food at once and died.

Again—urban legend—I have no idea if this story was true or if dogs even do this . . . not the point.

What I do remember is this story felt relatable AF. "I'm like that dog," I remember thinking. I was deep in my bulimia at this time, and any meal was an opportunity to go full-on binge. Once I started, I couldn't stop.

There's something very primal in a binge. The endorphin rush is real, and the more you consume, the longer you keep it going. Why eat a bowl of ice cream when I can enjoy a gallon? Why buy a donut when I can get a baker's dozen?

As many of you know, my eating disorder later morphed into substance use disorder. It was much easier to manage and less time consuming to sip cabernet while I parented. Call it "mommy juice" and no one bats an eyelash.

Author Gretchen Rubin talks about two personality types she's studied: the abstainer and the moderator. Some people can eat a fun-size Snickers and stop, and others (like me) need to avoid it or they will eat 12 of them (no exaggeration).

I am an abstainer because some things I'm simply not capable of moderating. Certain foods and booze.

I read a quote the other day: "It's a lot easier to not drink than it is to keep trying to stop drinking." (Jolene Park)

I feel that in my bones. I don't drink anymore because it's easier. Sobriety has many benefits: it's fulfilling, it's beautiful, and it's empowering. But at the end of the day, it's just plain easier.

I somehow have to tie this all back to the poor dog, don't I? Ok, here goes . . . binging, or drinking a glass of wine and craving more, more, more . . . primal instincts are behind these. We have evolved over thousands of years to seek out pleasure, to crave the endorphin rush.

It's how we've survived as a species.

If you have an abstainer mindset, you are not broken. There's a reason your body craves more. When we were hunting and gathering we ate everything we could get our hands on because tomorrow was unknown.

There was no Costco, people.

Put down the shame—it doesn't serve you. Seek a solution instead. Keep booze out of your house, tell your partner your plans not to drink, buy some quit-lit, and set yourself up to succeed. You can and you will. Because as humans we have also evolved to be incredibly resilient. We are built to do hard things. And if I have to be the poor dog in this analogy to get the point across, I will be.

I wish I could say that on the day I decided to quit I simply woke up refreshed from a good night's sleep and realized sobriety was where it was at. Alas, it wasn't so easy.

My story starts on a melancholy Monday the week before Christmas. Weeks of holiday party hangovers were already under my belt, and I was just getting started. The holidays were especially triggering for me, as all my family comes to town and the beer tap opens and champagne bottles start popping.

That day at work, I sat at my computer nursing a subtle hangover. Hangovers were common for me at this point, more of a nuisance, really, but certainly no excuse not to be productive. If anything, it was a push to increase my productivity, to prove that alcohol did not control me and that I still had full control over my life and my actions. Which, looking back, is a joke because anyone could tell you they are more productive without a headache and fuzzy concentration. No rocket science there.

The holidays make great excuses to drink. According to the Distilled Spirits Council of the United States, seasonal binge drinking is not uncommon and accounts for a quarter of the $49-billion-a-year profit for the distilled spirits industry between Thanksgiving and New Year's.[1] It's the perfect storm of visiting friends and family, parties, cold weather keeping us indoors, and the magic of the holidays and excitement of a new year ahead. And for regular drinkers, these circumstances simply give us excuses for drinking earlier and more.

This particular weekend, we had juggled three holiday parties in a two-day weekend. One was for business networking, and two were social occasions with friends. The drinking was heavy at all three parties, one even included an ice luge (something I hadn't seen since college), and when I tried to show reserve in my consumption—citing the pain that comes from parenting with a hangover—someone had suggested lacing my coffee with Tuaca. While I normally steered clear of hard liquor—one of my "fool's rules"—a few sips to stave off a headache from the previous day's partying seemed brilliant.

DAY ONE

All in all, it had been a pretty unremarkable weekend. I'd awakened that Monday with a moderate headache but no nausea, which I considered a small victory—until the moment I sat in my office chair and felt my heart flutter. Was it just me, or was my heart skipping beats? I put my hand to my chest to feel it better. Bu-dum . . . bu-dum . . . *pause* . . . bu-dum. Sweat lined my brow. That can't be right.

Panic set in quickly. I knew something was very wrong, and I was certain, thanks to my vast WebMD search experience, that I knew what it was. I was having a stroke. I was thirty-eight years old and I was having a stroke.

This sounds like an extreme reaction, I know. However, it's important to remember that my father suffered from a debilitating stroke at fifty-two. And although he did not die that day, he was permanently disabled and remained that way until his death at seventy-six.

When my dad had his stroke, it forever shaped my life and my understanding of alcoholism. Not in the "Oh my God, my dad is an alcoholic and I'd better be careful" way, but more of a "Wow, alcoholism is really dangerous, but it won't affect me until I'm at least fifty, so I don't have to worry about this for a long time" way that only our younger, dumber selves can rationalize so easily.

But when I felt those palpitations, thirty-eight and fifty-two felt like a small gap in age. Too small.

I rushed myself to the ER, knowing very well I probably should not be driving, given my symptoms. I was woozy and slightly nauseous now, and my heart was racing as I considered the possibility: a stroke. A stroke. A stroke.

I checked myself in and told the nurse my symptoms. Trouble breathing. Heart pounding. "It's a stroke . . ." I mumbled. The nurse took my vitals and ran a few tests. Then she sent me to the waiting room.

I texted my mom. "Please meet me at the ER. Something's wrong." She arrived forty-five minutes later, as I still waited.

At that point, it had become quite clear this wasn't a stroke or a heart attack. I was pretty sure the doctor would have seen me quickly if that had been a possibility. In the meantime, my heart had settled down. My breathing was stable again.

I knew that if there was ever a time to tell someone what had been on my mind for years, it was now. This drinking thing? I was losing control. What started as fun, what at first felt freeing and simple, was now the complete opposite. It was a heavy, heavy load of guilt, temptation, regret, and pain. This wasn't what I wanted for my life. This wasn't the kind of mom I wanted to be.

"Mom," I whispered, looking down at the white tile floor. "I think I have a drinking problem."

That was and is and always will be the moment that will define the start of my journey. These words spoken to that person.

I knew as soon as the words crossed my lips that I was altering the course of everything from that moment forward.

Unconsciously, I had been waiting years to share this secret with someone but also holding out for more time. Maybe my drinking story wasn't over just yet. Maybe I still had a few years in me. I wanted to release the weight of this secret, but I also knew the responsibility that came with it. By speaking the words out loud, I'd chartered a new course in my story. I'd spoken the truth of my troubles for my own ears finally to hear for the first time.

This wasn't the end. This was just the beginning. And it turned out that saying these momentous words was the easy part. The work was just getting started.

THE FIRST WEEK

When I think about that first week of sobriety, it's hard even to gather my thoughts. While I did not experience medical detox, the mental exhaustion felt like I was breathing out of a straw and left me with a deep fog clouding my memory of that week. I remember minutes passed like hours and days felt like years. Distraction and staying busy were key to getting through it, and that is the goal. No one in the history of recovery will ever tell you to savor that first week. Just get through it, and remember that this can perhaps be your last first week sober, well, ever!

Knowing what I know now, I would have sought out support immediately, either through AA or through another support program. These days, resources are widely available. It's not hard to find in-person or virtual options that meet your needs, your belief systems, and your learning styles.

But those first few days, AA did not feel like an option to me. Why? Because "I'm NoT aN AlCoHoLiC." I cringe writing this, but it's true that I was not willing to accept that label, even if it meant I'd be offered help.

In fact, I still struggle with the word "alcoholic." I know it's a useful and validating word for many, but watching my father drown in his own alcoholism and then using that same word to describe my own nuanced experience did not feel supportive or clarifying to me at all. My drinking felt nothing like my father's, so why would our labels overlap?

Health care professionals also do not use "alcoholic" as a clinical term. They do not diagnose someone as an alcoholic; instead, they refer to someone's inability to stop or control their alcohol use as a medical condition, called alcohol use disorder

(AUD). AUD is defined as a spectrum and encompasses alcohol abuse, alcohol dependence, and alcohol addiction. Considered a brain disorder, someone's AUD can be diagnosed as mild, moderate, or severe.[2]

And I'm not alone. I know "alcoholic" is a label that keeps many people from seeking help. Gray-area drinkers, for example. A gray-area drinker is defined as a person who drinks somewhere between socially and severely abusing alcohol. According to the website Gray Tonic, a gray-area drinker has not experienced a "rock bottom" or a major life-altering impact.[3] It's a label I'm far more comfortable standing behind than the word "alcoholic." I hear other people say this same thing all the time, almost daily. But just because a person isn't ready to commit to a label, that does not make them any less in need of support.

Without support and still largely unsure about how to describe my relationship with alcohol, I did the only thing I thought I could: I white knuckled it like my life depended on it. I kept my plan to stop drinking private, only telling John and my mom. I pretended to drink on Christmas and the days leading up to it, clutching a glass of wine and willing myself not to even hold it up to my nose to inhale the bouquet of dark fruit and florals, a habit I acquired over the years. At the time it seemed important, critical even, that this be a secret. The only thing that seemed worse than not drinking was being called out for not drinking. I couldn't face the shame of people noticing I wasn't drinking and drawing their own conclusions.

This is the stigma of addiction. It can paralyze a person from doing what is best and opt for the more frequented path instead. But I wasn't aware of anyone who didn't drink because it didn't serve them. There were only two camps of drinking that I knew: those who drank and those who couldn't. Everyone I knew either drank because, well, of course they did, or they had crossed the invisible line of addiction and were doomed to spend the rest of their lives struggling just to stay above water. I didn't know about that gray, middle area between moderate and problematic drinking where one drink wasn't enough but you haven't driven your car into a utility pole or gotten arrested at a cousin's wedding just yet.

Have a couple glasses of wine—you deserve it.

Cheers to surviving another hard week.

I only drink on days that end in "day."

I ate up these sayings with gusto, even as my hangovers became progressively worse. Even as I started to get regular panic attacks. Even as a normal visit to the doctor would show surprise results on my blood pressure. "Is your blood pressure normally so high?" "It might have to do with the six glasses of wine I had yesterday," I'd say . . . then we'd both laugh and move on.

When does problematic drinking stop becoming a funny story and become a real danger? Just because I never got a DUI or experienced a stroke doesn't make my drinking any less of a problem than it is for someone who is drinking the exact same amount as I am and suffers severe physical consequences. Regardless of outcome, my drinking was still "high risk," a.k.a. more than three drinks a day for women, according to the National Institute on Alcohol Abuse and Alcoholism (NIAAA).[4]

For every raging alcoholic, there are countless people who are drinking problematically. I think about some of my drinking buddies who are still high-risk drinkers but who do not define themselves as having a drinking problem.

When will they see it as a problem? Maybe never. Or maybe they have a health scare or get an ultimatum from a family member. Or maybe they get no warning at all and their body finally gives up.

I did not write anything during that first week. Recently I checked my social media from that time to get a feeling for my headspace then, and I didn't post anything that week. It was like I'd crawled into a hole and hid myself away, waiting for the courage to come back out.

I do recall the constant head games, and I've heard of similar experiences from others. The mind tricks telling us this is stupid and unnecessary. Watching others drink and thinking they drink just as much as we do, so why do we have to stop? Feeling sorry for ourselves and believing alcohol really will help us feel better.

"New sobriety is a fingernail on the blackboard experience," Ann Dowsett Johnston says.[5] You would think our bodies would want sobriety. And they do. Our bodies expend so much energy trying to take care of us, even as we sabotage them at every turn. But our heads have other plans. And this first week? Our mind is our worst enemy. My inner voice sounded something like this:

You can start this next week. It's been a hard day. Try this tomorrow. You went two days without a drink last week. Obviously, you don't have a problem.
Everyone else is drinking. Why can't you?

On and on and on my mind would fill with constant chatter, trying to throw me off my game to stop drinking altogether. Honestly, I look back now and realize it was a miracle I got through it. I probably didn't write anything for fear I would convince myself not to go through with it. I believed I couldn't trust myself. Basically, I've spent my whole life believing that.

But after that first day of sobriety—Day 1—I told myself, "I never have to do that again." Each day I reminded myself that another day was over. I would never have to do it again. And that was my "trick" for getting through that first week. Promising myself that by sticking it out, I was one day closer to freedom. Because every day gets easier. Every day feels freer.

What made my first week exponentially harder was my decision to tackle this on my own. Instead of getting support and love, people were unknowingly testing me with every offer to get me a drink, with holding their wine glass close enough that I could smell the fruity aroma without knowing I was hanging on to early sobriety by a thread.

In that first week, I didn't yet know what my long-term plans were. Is this forever? Is this just a test? Do I have a problem, or do I just need to get better at moderation?

So I lied. I told people I was sick. Or I was doing a cleanse. I had to assure a few people I wasn't pregnant, but even so, having someone suspect I was pregnant was preferable to having them think I had a drinking problem.

If I could go back and do that first week all over again, here's what I would do:

1. I would check in with my general practitioner to make sure I could safely quit cold turkey or if I needed help to medically detox and get tips on how to alleviate the discomfort.

2. I would read *This Naked Mind* and *Quit Like a Woman*, both books that emphasize the harmful nature of alcohol and

why it makes quitting so damn hard for *everyone*, not just "alcoholics."

3. I would find a community, either through AA or through the myriad of other programs out there.

4. I would search Facebook for one of the many supportive, private communities for sober women.

5. I would avoid parties or any social gatherings that involved alcohol (since I quit over Christmas, this would have been decidedly harder).

6. I would have set more boundaries. I think I was so afraid of shaking up the status quo that I inadvertently said yes to showing up at more events, parties, and after work obligations than were necessary. My family would have been fine if I'd opted out of things that made me uncomfortable, and John wouldn't have cared if I told him leaving open wine bottles around after dinner parties triggered me. But in the back of my mind, I didn't want my husband or my mom to realize just how big a deal this was for me. I had done such a good job keeping this part of me secret, to reveal how vulnerable and scared I really was meant admitting just how big a pickle I was in. And I wasn't ready to go there. Not yet.

THE FIRST THIRTY DAYS

The only day I remember with clarity during those first few weeks is New Year's Eve. We agreed to join some friends at a nice restaurant that night and I was frantic. These were drinking buddies of ours and it would just be five of us, so there would be no way to hide my drink selection.

I was less than two weeks sober at this point, so while I had gotten through the hump of the incredibly challenging first week, this would be my first test outside of my family and in such small company.

As one of our friends started reviewing the wine list, I could feel my heart beating like a drummer in a marching band. Here it comes . . .

"What does everyone want to drink?"

I held off, letting everyone speak first. Maybe they won't even get to me. But when all eyes turned to me, I said softly, "Nothing for me. I'm good with water."

That was it. I wasn't booted out of our booth or chastised or smirked at, but my friend next to me quietly asked why, trying not to make it a whole table conversation.

"I'm not pregnant or anything." I felt like I needed to nip that assumption in the bud. "I'm just taking a break."

She left it at that for a few minutes until the bottles of wine they had ordered arrived at the table. But then she said something I'll never forget. "You picked a bad night to not drink." She was referring to the fancy wine they ordered, of course. And I remember screaming inside at the unfairness of it all. Everyone at this table enjoyed booze just as much as I did. How is it they get to enjoy classy wine in froufrou goblets while I get stuck with ice water all night?

I considered saying, "Screw it." In fact, looking back I'm both humbled and incredibly proud of the fact that I didn't cave. The sober app I use to track my sober time (I use the free version of I Am Sober) sends me an inspirational message every day at 10:00 a.m. My favorite message has always been "You didn't come this far only to come this far." Perhaps that was what kept me strong that night at the dinner table. I recognized that I never had to be on day fourteen of my sobriety ever again. If I could get through this hurdle—and there would always be hurdles—I could see day fifteen, day twenty-one, and soon, day thirty.

I didn't come this far only to come this far.

There are many ways to quit drinking, and so many books and research articles on the topic, many of which I've referenced in this book. Here I want to focus on a few things that I've learned from having heard many stories over the years from other women who've struggled.

First of all, there is no shame in going to inpatient or outpatient rehabilitation, and it's a more common choice than you might expect. I've seen and heard about complete transformations from so many women who say that thirty, sixty, or even more days with professionals was exactly what they needed. In fact, insurance often covers at least part of it.

As mothers, it might seem unimaginable—selfish even—to take off to rehab and leave our families. For many, it may feel impossible. But consider the alternative. If you're willing to dig deep and see the black hole your drinking is dragging you toward, taking some time to go all-in on your recovery could make the difference between life and death. Thirty days compared to death seems a hell of a lot more reasonable. If you believe rehab would be the best option for you to turn your life around, do not let shame or social stigma stop you. And if it's the potential cost that's holding you back, talk to your doctor. They might steer you toward other options to ensure that you detox safely. Your health insurance provider or nonprofits offering free support could be valuable resources as well.

Maybe you're reading this thinking, "No. Rehab isn't even close to where I'm at right now. I'm not even sure I have a problem." No worries, I've got you. Anyone who chooses to quit drinking should do so on their own terms. What's important is to do what you think will work for you. I encourage you to find a support group that feels right and meets your needs. There are tons of different types of meetings to choose from—both in person and virtual. AA, She Recovers, and Sober Mom Squad all offer free sober meetings just for women.

I think most of us are familiar with the 12-step program AA uses in their recovery process. It is a vetted, well-respected, and widely practiced program that many explore as they begin their sober journey. But there are alternatives if you are interested. Annie Grace's This Naked Mind community runs a thirty-day "Alcohol Experiment" with paid and free options. The SMART recovery model (Self-Management and Recovery Training) is distinctly different than 12-steps and steers clear of AA's faith-based approach.

For those who aren't quite sure they're ready to quit but want to understand their relationship with alcohol better, Dr. Anna Lembke offers an interesting approach in her book, *Dopamine Nation*.[6] Dopamine is a brain chemical that can provide an intense feeling of reward or pleasure. Since dopamine is a natural neurotransmitter that affects our ability to strive, focus, and plan, too much of it can have a seriously negative effect. Dr. Lembke suggests dopamine fasting as a way to neutralize any behaviors triggered by an overconsumption of high dopamine substances. This isn't just drugs or alcohol, but even an overreliance on phones, TV, or gaming, which all contribute to dopamine over-stimulation. The steps she lays out are quite simple and follow the acronym DOPAMINE:

D—Data

Collect the basic facts about your consumption: What/where/when do you use this "substance"?

O—Objectives

Understand the why. What purpose does the behavior serve?

P—Problems

What problems is the behavior causing?

A—Abstinence

Lembke recommends abstaining from the behavior for at least thirty days to reset our pleasure-pain balance, and gives suggestions about how to do that. Our body desires homeostasis, so when we feel intense feelings of pleasure or pain, our body will work to self-regulate our feelings back to equilibrium.

M—Mindfulness

Observe what your brain is doing while it's cutting back on the behavior. This is the key to the fasting.

I—Insight

Abstinence gives us clarity into our behaviors that we don't notice when we are using/doing.

N—Next Steps

Determine what you want to do after your thirty days of fasting are over. Can you return to the substance/behavior and moderate it better? In some cases, such as drug and alcohol use, you might recognize that you don't want to go back to the old habit and are loving this wave you're riding. For other things, like phones or sugar, abstinence might be harder to achieve, so you must determine a new approach that allows you to use it less or more mindfully.

E—Experiment

Through trial and error, it's time to figure out what works and what doesn't. Can you effectively moderate? Do you want to keep going? Learn what works for you.[7]

Whatever kind of support you want to lean on to get you through the first thirty days, the best practice is "A" for abstinence in all of them. While I think it's safe to say the first thirty days are probably the hardest on this journey, they are also the most important. These thirty days are setting you on an entirely new trajectory. Your brain is being rewired and your habits transformed. You start day one questioning everything, but you reach day thirty feeling like you can do anything.

Of course, for some people even the idea of one day let alone thirty feels unattainable. While abstinence is obviously more optimal than just reducing use, research shows that harm reduction is a safer alternative to no change at all.[8] Harm reduction means different things to different people, so I want to clarify that I define it as working to cut down on your alcohol use enough to eliminate problems or provide valuable data.

Harm reduction will provide you with one of three outcomes: (1) you are able to cut down enough to eliminate problems, thus successfully reducing both problems and intake; (2) you are unable to cut down enough to eliminate problems, thus providing valuable information about your lack of control; and (3) you cut down and the experience prompts you to stop altogether.

Harm reduction is controversial, as some see it as enabling or distracting people from the better option of abstinence. Honestly, I get it. I debated even including it in the book at all. But the way I see it is, my attempts at moderation were essentially my efforts toward harm reduction; I just didn't know it at the time. And it did work in a way because through experimenting with moderation, I learned that I cannot control my alcohol use.

If you have tried and failed at moderating your alcohol in the past, then you can also find valuable data from that information. You can recognize moderation is not an option and abstinence is your ultimate goal. If taking alcohol completely off the table makes you sad or angry to hear, you are not alone. I went through the five stages of grief (denial, anger, bargaining, depression, acceptance) when realizing moderation wouldn't work for me. Take heart though that these feelings are temporary. This short period of discomfort will lead to long-term feelings of freedom and peace.

THE FIRST YEAR

After my first month sober, my mom connected me to a biking friend of hers who she knew was in AA. I agreed to meet Penny (not her real name) at a nearby coffee shop because I didn't know anyone who'd deliberately gotten sober and I had some questions about quitting alcohol for good, AA, and how to approach sobriety as an opportunity, not a consequence. Penny talked about hitting her rock bottom with alcohol and later with drugs, and I remember thinking that she and I didn't have much in common. I still wasn't even sure I had a drinking problem, and Penny had been shooting heroin in front of her kids. I felt like we were living on different planets, and I emotionally distanced her problems from my own immediately.

Penny suggested for me to try an AA meeting and I told her I was a mom—who would watch my kids while I attended meetings? (Of course, John would have been happy to watch the kids. I think the real issue was I didn't want John to know I was struggling enough to go to meetings in the first place.) Penny said at the very least I should read the Big Book, the basic text of AA that lays out the main principles in their approach to recovery.

Before we parted I had one big question for her: I was going on a big trip to Mexico with my husband for our fifth anniversary in a few months. It's an "all you can drink" booze fest. Did she think it would be OK to take a week off, like a vacation from sobriety, and then go right back to it? We'd planned the vacation before I quit drinking, and half the reason we'd chosen this trip was for endless piña coladas. Our rooms even had liquor dispensers in the cabinets.

She looked at me for a long time. I imagine she was trying hard to maintain her composure as she added this to her list of "dumb questions the newly sober ask."

Penny told me that no, I could not just opt out of my sobriety for a few days and call it good. She said that my days would start back at the beginning when I was ready to get back on track. What really resonated with me was when she said that if I was going to make an exception for this, it would be increasingly easy for me to make more and more exceptions in the future.

She was right. I knew myself well enough to recognize that's exactly what I would do. A trip to Mexico followed by an epic 4th of July party. By Christmas, I would be restarting my clock every weekend.

I did read the Big Book, as Penny suggested. It didn't resonate for me, but in retrospect, I think I could have brought to it a more open-minded approach, and it might have given me more context if I'd gone to some AA meetings. I recognize that now and hope to explore the book and the founding principles again one day. But at the time, maybe my father's experience still felt too raw, too emotional, and too hopeless for me to genuinely come into the rooms of AA with an open heart. I'd seen my dad attend AA for years. I often drove him there and picked him up when he was in town to visit me. He would collect chips commemorating thirty days, sixty days, ninety days of sobriety, and all the while he would still drink. The hypocrisy of that made me angry, which was no fault of the AA program, but in addiction, blame often overlaps with underlying emotions, like the ocean tide along a sandy shore.

I remember one time when I was waiting outside a meeting for my dad, and when he didn't come out, I walked inside to find him passed out in a chair in the hallway. As I went to help lift him up, someone walked by and said, "He's been there the whole time. I don't know why he even bothered coming." I said nothing but inside I felt embarrassed, defensive, and angry.

My dad wanted more than anything to do the right thing, but his addiction was killing him from within. This was just one among countless moments of pain, disappointment, embarrassment, and heartbreak—all stemming from his addiction. Hoping for the best but settling for the worst. It took so much from me, from my dad, from our family. All I wanted was for people to see him and understand. To see me and offer a hand. But that day, as with so many days in our lives, it felt like my dad was just another drunk in someone else's way.

Between my father's history with AA, my very limited experience with Penny, and reading the Big Book, I wanted to chart a different course to sobriety for myself. I needed to find a place I felt like I could belong to figure it all out.

I often wonder how my sobriety would have changed if I'd embraced AA. It is the most popular and well-known recovery program in the world, after all. I have many friends now who credit AA as the reason they are still alive. I often get messages or comments from strangers who tell me that by not embracing the twelve steps, I'm doomed to relapse. While I believe AA is an impactful, substantial recovery program for many, I firmly believe it's *not* the only way to recover.

Both my kids were in a private day care/preschool by the time I quit drinking. My oldest was three years old and starting to show some unusual behaviors that the school would alert us to but told us not to worry about. The teacher assured us it would pass with time and maturity, but we experienced power struggles and meltdowns at home that felt alarming and kept us on our toes.

In April, the school principal called us for an emergency meeting. My husband and I walked in like deer in headlights, with no heads up on the topic nor who we were meeting. The principal and the teachers of our two kids sat around a boardroom table to recount an incident at school that morning when our youngest came to school with soiled underwear. They accused us of supposed negligence, offering a number of other examples. Like one time when Kevin had marker on his arms that remained for over a week (he had gotten his hands on a permanent marker). Or how the boys sometimes arrived at the car drop-off line with food on their faces. "Do you let your kids eat *in the car?*" the principal had asked, aghast. Um, yes. Was that unusual?

The principal called this a wakeup call. "Wake up!" she reiterated with a loud clap of her hands. But I was wide awake. I had been sober more than four months at that point, and I knew my husband and I were being completely gaslighted. Our kids were not machines, they were kids, and we were not robots, we were imperfect parents. Our kids ran around barefoot, loved to eat with their hands, and fought tooth and nail when we wiped their faces. Could we be better about cleaning up when they left the car at school? Yes. Were we going to stop letting them play in the sandbox before school because they showed up with sand in their hair on occasion? Nope.

That day will go down as one of the most humiliating, heartbreaking days of my life. I'm embarrassed even to mention it because I immediately feel the need to defend our parenting and care for our children. But I bring it up for a very important reason. I often wonder if that experience would have broken me had I not been sober at the time.

But to have this meeting months into my steady sobriety, I could stand by my actions with confidence. I knew their complaints were BS. Did John and I have work to do to be better parents? Absolutely. Did it warrant an on-the-spot shame storm that left me weeping for days and my husband in a spiral of rage? Not at all.

It was the first time sobriety saved me. But it would not be the last.

Five months into my sobriety, I took the Mexican trip I had told Penny about. As I packed for this preplanned booze fest following the hardest, most painful week of my life, everything felt wrong. Wrong venue. Wrong timing. Wrong mindset.

So much of me wanted to just lean into this vacation. Forget the past five months and everything it took to get me there. It felt like a mistake to be leaving the kids after such heinous accusations from the school, and John and I talked at length about canceling the trip. While the situation at school left both of us devastated, I believe parent shaming has a greater impact on moms than dads in general. In part, it's due to many men's ability to compartmentalize their thoughts and feelings while many women carry everything at once like an internet browser with dozens of tabs constantly up and running.

It's also due to gender expectations in parenting. Is there a worse thing to call a woman than a bad mom? I can't think of anything more painful or degrading. It's a slander I would wish on no one. Dads don't feel that same pressure; in fact, many would argue the opposite. There are so little expectations for fathers, even in modern times, that just watching a dad hustling around a grocery store with a few kids in tow or a dad mindfully spending time with his kids at a playground tends to warrant coos and praise. "You're such a good father!" "Dad's day with the kids!" I remember seeing a meme in which a woman's mother said, "It's so nice of your husband to watch the kids so much," and her daughter retorting, "Yes, Mom, it's great that he continues to be a parent to his own children."

Recently, I've become aware of a name for this: "Dad privilege." It's the term one woman, whose TikTok handle is @Cloebluffcakes, uses to describe when her husband does the same errands she does with the kids, but he's treated like a hero. "Like a hero!" she reiterates in her video.[9] The video earned 1.3 million likes and nearly twenty thousand comments, many from other mothers sharing relatable experiences.

In general, it seems like men have a lot less to lose when someone criticizes or judges their parenting, probably because the expectations we set for them in that arena are just that much lower. That being said, John was deeply hurt over our school experience, but he believed getting away for a week might give us the space to really process events and get clarity on what we do next. And he was right. But he wasn't aware of all the reasons for my hesitation. The allure of the alcohol all around us terrified me, but I feared opening up to him about it. In my heart I still wasn't sure what would come from this new sober journey of mine. What if I revealed my fears and then ended up going back to drinking?

People ask me if John also quit drinking during this time to support my sobriety. And as you can probably guess, I never gave him a reason to think I needed his support. I worried my newfound sobriety would impact our relationship because alcohol always played a central role in weekends, family events, and vacations during our relationship. I wanted to downplay this as just a casual change, like trying a plant-based diet or switching to sugar-free creamer.

Fears over the impact of quitting alcohol on a relationship are a major concern for many. One of the most common questions I get asked is how to navigate a relationship where the other partner is still drinking. Harder still? A relationship where the partner doesn't support your sobriety (which happens more often than you might think). While John was supportive of my decision to quit drinking, I hear many stories of women who either feel pressured to drink or watch firsthand as their former drinking buddy continues to spiral into the painful descent of addiction. What then?

It's a question I asked Annie Grace, author of *This Naked Mind*, in an Instagram live.[10] Grace said the pressure comes from a place of fear. A partner might think, "I'm being left behind. You're evolving past me." Like so many others, we don't even know what our relationship would look like without alcohol, so it makes sense that this change would feel like scary, unchartered territory for a couple.

Grace encourages people to chart their own sober course and let their experience lead by example. Refrain from pressuring your partner to join you and acknowledge that this is your decision, not theirs. AA uses the saying, "Attraction, not promotion." Oftentimes, a partner will see the other person blossom and thrive, and they will naturally get curious. If not, consider the implications for the relationship and for your children if both of you remained in a toxic drinking cycle.

Amanda White also suggests that you have early conversations with your partner around setting boundaries. "Come up with what [your] nonnegotiable boundaries are. It could be different for everyone. Maybe they don't want alcohol in the house, or they don't want to go to a bar."[11] Then determine where there might be wiggle room. If your partner wants alcohol in the house, can they keep it in the garage or another space where it's not in your face?

I didn't have any of these conversations with John. We didn't have any hard alcohol in the house anyway, and I tried to ignore the beer and wine. I did pour a few open bottles of wine down the drain after parties instead of putting them in the fridge and sent a few home with guests on occasion too. I didn't find alcohol in the house all that triggering because I remembered that for me, it was never about having just one. I would "play the tape through," a common recovery phrase, which means consider the full experience of where that first sip would lead. This was a powerful strategy that helped me overcome countless cravings.

Anyway, we went to Mexico, and I stuck to my guns. I kept recalling the school experience and how going back to drinking would only compromise all the work I was doing to not be a crappy mom. By doubling down on my sobriety, I wasn't letting the school administrator win.

That week was hard, there is no tiptoeing around it. We might have been sitting on a beach in paradise, but I was squirming every moment of that trip. Every time John ordered a cocktail, every time I looked in the TV console where the liquor dispensers lived, and with every "Can I get you a drink, senorita?" I clenched my teeth and shook my head.

But it wasn't all mental war games. I would wake up early in the morning and go to the hotel gym, something I'd never done on vacation before. I would come back to the room feeling invigorated and refreshed while John was still in bed. I admit I watched curiously as other vacationers ordered drinks, and I was fascinated by their drinking habits. I'd assumed everyone was getting as drunk as I was, but here, many people were slowly sipping one, maybe two drinks. Apparently not everyone was out to get blitzed every chance they got. As I observed that others were perfectly happy without tracking down a server for yet another one, or spending hours at the bar, I wondered how I must have looked when inebriated. All the ridiculous, cringy things I'd laughed off, believing everyone else in the room was just as drunk as I was. Because from what I was starting to see, it wasn't nearly as many as I'd thought. The experience only affirmed for me that I was making the right choice by pursuing sobriety.

When I got home from that week in Mexico, I felt like I'd won the sober Olympics. I'd done it; I'd gotten through the greatest test of my sobriety to date and I was so damn proud of myself. Sobriety is beautifully rewarding in ways active drinking can never be. It's catching a moment you would have missed if you were constantly focused on getting the waiter's attention. It's waking up in the morning feeling clear headed and optimistic. It's having a conversation with someone that genuinely interests you, and not just a way to kill time while you down your drink or think about how to bow out to get a refill.

I always considered myself a fun-loving party girl but when booze is off the table, it turns out parties are decidedly awkward for me. Walking into an acquaintance's house just for small talk with random people for hours? Maybe I wasn't as extroverted as

I'd thought. And maybe the parties and the social outings were more about the opportunities to drink than anything else.

I was thirty-nine years old at this point and learning things about myself I'd never known, never thought to question. When you talk to people who want advice on quitting drinking, a common concern is how they'll have fun without alcohol. The best answer I can give is that sobriety offers an entirely new definition of fun. Now I see that parties weren't really fun for me at all. They were just opportunities to drink without feeling scrutinized. Another similar question is, "What if *I'm* not fun without alcohol?" If being fun for your friends means acting differently than who you are at your core, then maybe those people aren't really friends.

Look, I'm not going to beat around the bush, since I stopped drinking I can be a real buzz kill at parties. I started doing what Catherine Gray calls the "trapdoor technique,"[12] which is when someone just ups and leaves a party without saying goodbye. People find it rude, but in this first year of my sobriety, it was a tool I used to opt out when I was feeling uncomfortable or triggered. Do you think my *real* friends care if I have to jump ship without walking around doing goodbye hugs at parties? Nope.

With the vacation behind us, John and I made some important decisions on the home front. We pulled our kids out of the preschool and started mapping out the options available in our area. As I started gathering recommendations from other parents, I found that the school we'd left had a reputation for not only "waking up" other parents, they also were well known for booting kids out for all sorts of frivolous reasons. That made me even more assured in the changes we were making, and again, so grateful to not be doing it through the fog of hangovers and hangxiety.

One of the unspoken and beautiful benefits of sobriety is that it just keeps getting easier. Summers are full of drinking pressure, from camping, to Fourth of July, to beaches or lake trips. It amuses me now how my friends and I couldn't seem to enjoy the great outdoors without tying it to alcohol. I specifically remember a fun boat trip with some friends that turned me upside down when everyone started popping open bottles of beer. I couldn't do a trapdoor exit on a speedboat, but boy, did I want to. That trigger hit me out of nowhere. I'd never realized how firmly my brain was wired to automatically connect alcohol with certain activities. And now I had to go through each one without that connection. The first boat ride without. The first camping trip without. The first baseball game or concert without. Any activity you'd connected to alcohol in the past is likely to trigger you, which is why it's so important to be prepared.

"Exposure therapy" is an important and useful means of adjusting to fears, triggers, and breaking habits. I first heard the term on the *Sober Powered* podcast where the host, Gill Tietz, discussed going to her first wedding sober, and she talked about how scared she was of how triggering the experience might be. The American Psychological Association describes exposure therapy as a behavior modification strategy used in psychological treatment to help people confront their fears. While there are several variations of it, ultimately, it's the practice of exposing someone to what they fear and helping them desensitize from the situation or object.[13]

As you can imagine, with continued exposure to your fears, you start to recognize a situation as less dangerous, and it becomes easier to endure each and every time. It's something every person in sobriety will have to experience in one way or another, unless they shut themselves out of social situations completely, which is hardly a healthy way to live.

After the wedding, Gill described feeling relieved and gleeful that she did what she set out to do—not drink. And I know the feeling well. It's how I felt on New Year's Eve at dinner with my friends. It's how I felt attending a Journey cover band concert with drinking buddies, and yes—it's how I felt camping and going on that speed boat for the first time. It turned out that to feel that rush of accomplishment from sticking to your goal and overcoming an obstacle is far more rewarding than any drink. And it's liberating to know that we *do* get rewarded in sobriety: every day we have the gift of a growing sense of relief and self-assurance in the commitment we've made (not to mention the lack of a hangover).

SHARING THE JOURNEY

By the time fall came, I started feeling more settled into my new sober lifestyle. Getting through summer had been a huge milestone, and I felt less vulnerable and fearful about the "what" and "how" that were ahead. I still hadn't told anyone besides John and my mom, but it was less because I was worried about the stigma and more that having a problem with alcohol didn't seem like something I should be proud of. Why would anyone want to know I was sober?

Then someone in a writers' group I participated in started a Facebook thread of things that made us proud of ourselves and invited us to pat ourselves on the back so the group could cheer us on too. Some women wrote about parenting victories, others touted personal accomplishments. Jodie Utter, author of the blog Utter Imperfection, surprised me by commenting with obvious delight that she was six weeks sober and feeling great.

Wait . . . what? Her honesty and lack of shame in vocalizing sobriety publicly struck me. I didn't know Jodie personally, but I loved her wit and voice, and as a virtual writing sister, she connected to me deeply. I could tell in her post that she was eager to share this news with our group of women.

I was eleven months sober at the time and had been writing publicly for a few years, mostly about motherhood. After seeing Jodie's post, something hit me like a lightning bolt. This sobriety journey was a positive thing, nothing to be ashamed of. Why was I hiding it from the world like a stain when it has done nothing but turned my entire world around in a good way?

That December, I wrote a short piece on social media announcing I was one year sober. I worried what my readers might say, since it's a topic I'd never embarked on before. Sobriety was not my niche, and while I wasn't big on mommy wine memes, I certainly had shared a few over the years. But now I felt inspired to be vulnerable and speak up about it because I was proud of myself and I hoped it might resonate with others.

So on December 18, 2018, I posted the following on Facebook:

Today is a big day. It's the one-year anniversary of the day I decided I had enough. I put the bottle down. I sobered up.

What? You didn't know about my struggles with alcohol? Does this change your perspective of me? As a woman? As a mom?

This used to matter to me. What you thought about me used to mean everything. And in truth, it still does a little. I've kept this part of me under the radar for fear of judgment . . . shame . . . stigmatization.

I don't know a lot of things. I don't know how to stop at one drink. I don't know when to say, "No, thanks, I've had enough." But I do know I'm better off with nothing at all. I do know my family is stronger, happier and safer when I'm sober. I do know I can wake up fresh and hangover free. I do know my life is more enriched and beautiful when I'm sober.

Is it hard? Of course it is. There were so many tests this year. Breaking a 20+ year habit is hard. I used to drink when I was happy, I drank when I was sad. I drank when I was anxious and I drank when I was bored.

I drank to socialize. I drank to hide. I drank to numb. I drank to feel secure.

Now I don't drink at all. I've had to find other coping mechanisms. But I've also had to do it scared. I've had to feel the feelings . . . all the feelings I used to drink to escape from. I can no longer hide.

But this is life! This is what it's all about! It's feeling the feelings. It's doing the shit that scares you. It's feeling terrified and standing up and stepping out anyway.

Do you know what the greatest part about this past year has been? The release of guilt. The elimination of alcohol-related regret. I no longer wake up with regrets. I no longer look at my kids with the guilt of a mom who drinks to numb the stress of parenting. The stress of them. The stress of this life I have brought them into.

I'm no saint. I still do stupid shit. I yell at my kids. I lose it pretty often, actually. But to parent without the alcohol-fueled buzz? This is priceless to me. I'm a better mother without alcohol. I'm a better wife. I'm a better person.

Can you stop at just one drink? I envy you. Do you linger over your glass of wine and feel satisfied, and say "no, thanks" when you're offered more? I can only imagine. This is not me, and it will never be me. I will never reach a time or place where I can moderate my drinking. I know this now. It's been a long, harrowing journey, but I know this more than anything I've ever known.

I used to think alcohol served me in some way. It no longer does. It served a different person. A person who wasn't strong enough, wasn't ready to feel everything. To be everything. I'm not that girl anymore. I've never been stronger. I'm ready to feel again.

But I'm no superwoman. In many ways, I've never been weaker. I know alcohol is my kryptonite. I know I'm one drink away from a binge. I know I'm one poor decision away from a lifetime of regret. And I'm so weak, I know I cannot touch booze. I know I must feel again. I have to feel everything again.

I feel good today. Sobriety suits me. I don't feel good every day though, and I still double glance when the person next to me orders a cab or merlot. Maybe I always will. But I never want to go back to day one. I never want to start this journey over again. The first day of recovery is the hardest. Today is day 365, and every day gets better. I promise.

Do you struggle to stop at one? Do you know in your heart you have a problem but don't know where to start or when it's time? I have something amazing to tell you. You can change your life today . . . right now . . . for the better. Don't wait for rock bottom. Don't wait till your health deteriorates, or you drive your kids drunk somewhere, or your spouse leaves you. Beat alcohol to the punch and change your life today.

It will be the hardest day of your life. It will also be one of the greatest. It will be the day you decide to feel again. It will be the day you decide to take control back in your life. It will be the day you can see your kids and partner with a focus and intention you've never experienced before. You will never regret it.

I received hundreds of comments on the post. Hundreds of shares, too. Scary Mommy, a popular mom blogging site with millions of readers, asked to repost it. I was shocked. All this time I believed sobriety meant I had failed. But I had it all wrong. Sobriety was the outcome I didn't know I was even looking for, and it wasn't something to be ashamed of—it was something to celebrate.

I realized I want to share this journey out loud. If my story inspires one person, it will all be worth it. For the past year, I had been so focused on myself and my survival, I never stopped to think about how I could help others just by speaking about my experience. I wasn't a doctor or an addiction specialist, and I wasn't a therapist, but in telling my story, I could lift others and help end the stigma around addiction, recovery, and sobriety.

I have learned so much since I quit, most importantly how to trust myself. For the first time in my life, I have faith in the woman I am and the voice inside of me telling me who I am and why I matter. Alcohol lied to me for so many years, there was a time I didn't know *who* was speaking, Celeste or my alcohol use disorder. To be able to trust myself and my body again, there are no words to describe that metamorphosis in a person.

I also learned the beautiful skill of setting boundaries. I know what I will and will not put up with. I've learned to say no to people and things that are not beneficial or healthy. I've learned who is with me and who just liked me because I was a drinking buddy. Setting boundaries was a skill I could only learn in sobriety.

Lastly, something else happened when I reached a year that would forever shift my outlook. For the first time in my sober journey, I realized this is a long-term lifestyle I was ready and excited to accept. I wanted sobriety in my life every day and I was ready to commit. Done were my intrusive thoughts that maybe I would go back to drinking—that maybe this was just a short-term experiment. After 365 days hangover free, I knew with conviction this was the life for me and I was ready to look forward, not fall back.

LIGHTEN YOUR LOAD

♦ Find an accountability partner, someone who will not judge your reasons for quitting but who also won't let you off the hook down the road when you want to give into temptation. It might be a family member or friend or your therapist. This is a great way to lighten your load because early sobriety feels heavy if you carry it alone.

♦ Get a sober app and embrace the ways technology can help you through this. There are free sober apps that let you start tracking your days. I use the "I am sober" app. Every day it alerts me with a new motivational quote and I can pop in to look at the day's tally to see how far I've come whenever I could use some reinforcement. Also, Facebook has a ton of private sober groups that range from mom-focused to locally based. Check out a few and make sure they are supportive and motivational *and not* toxic or triggering. I even have one called "Alcohol Free

Living with Celeste Yvonne." Members find great relief in talking about things they're struggling with, as well as sharing tips and tricks that help them.

♦ Do some research. Understand the symptoms of PAWS (post-acute withdrawal symptoms), which affect some but not all with substance use disorder. Symptoms include anxiety, depression, insomnia, and chronic pain and can last up to two years.[14] Also, understanding typical changes that occur both physically and mentally during early sobriety, as well as some of the common causes of relapse, will help you stay strong when life happens (as it always does).

♦ Resources for sober living are massive. Gone are the days when AA is your only option. If you think AA is right for you, there's undoubtedly a group near you. Find it at aa.org. If you want other options, check out www.the temper.com/sober-communities-beyond-traditional-aa/.

♦ Check out some books. Books I've found extremely helpful in my sober journey include *This Naked Mind Control Alcohol* by Annie Grace (a game changer!), *The Sober Diaries* by Clare Pooley, *Sober for Good* by Anne Fletcher, and *The Unexpected Joy of Being Sober* by Catherine Gray. I've included more sober resources in the Resource Library at the end of this book.

♦ Although I didn't initially join a support community, it is the right choice for many. Isolating in early sobriety, while seemingly less triggering or scary, can sometimes be really lonely and uncomfortable. Does the community have to be sober-focused? Not necessarily, although I would recommend having a few sober contacts with whom you can get into the deeper aspects of the experience. Find a community of people who are only a text message or meeting away. You can do that through a sober group or through the Meetup app (they have sober groups). A nearby church is a great way to meet other moms.

◆ My social media followers' recommendations nailed it, as usual. Erin suggested attending meetings every single day, which ordinarily would be really hard for a mother of young ones, but all the new virtual options make it much more doable. Samantha suggests finding nonalcoholic drink options, and I highly agree. While some people find NA beer or wine triggering, triggers are different for us all. Figure out an NA option that works for you and have fun with it. Jess said she focused on her creative outlets that first year: writing and art. Having a creative outlet is so important. Maggie says she "celebrated each month's milestone," which can include going out for a pedicure or taking your favorite nature hike to help you strive for achievable goals. Emily said she did "yoga, journaling, and spent a lot of time at home with family. Also rested a lot." The truth is, you will feel really tired that first year because recovery is a lot of mental and emotional work! Give yourself that time and grace to rest when and where you can. Your body and your soul deserve it.

8 | I'M SOBER NOW. CAN WE STILL BE FRIENDS?

DESIREE'S STORY

"You really need to be brave, because you just keep losing yourself in this cycle," a therapist told Desiree, thirty-nine. Desiree sees her alcohol and drug issues as clearly tied back to childhood trauma. It was through the work with a therapist that she finally understood how she fell so far down the addiction cycle, which all came to a head during the pandemic, as it did for so many.

Desiree initially turned to drugs to help her escape from her chaotic family life, leaving home at eighteen and quickly developing a drug problem. She became a stripper to help pay the bills and cover her drug habit—soon getting pregnant with her high school sweetheart, who also struggled with drugs.

Desiree quit drugs cold turkey and tried to use her pregnancy to turn over a new leaf, but after her son was born, the reality of motherhood set in. The responsibility of caring for a baby while keeping a roof over their heads felt overwhelming, and she turned back to drugs.

Over the years, the cycle repeated, with Desiree trying to find ways to outrun drugs, and later, alcohol, but falling back into old coping mechanisms. She started a relationship with her now husband, who was against drugs but liked to drink, so Desiree transferred her drug use into just alcohol.

When the pandemic hit in 2020, Desiree became determined to stop drinking. It would be one thing if drinking actually helped, but it only made everything worse. Toxic relationships, the overwhelming nature of parenting, and day-to-day stressors snowballed Desiree's mental health to a dark place, and her alcohol-fueled lifestyle became unsustainable. Through therapy, Desiree realized how long she had been playing the victim and blaming others; now it was time to accept accountability.

Desiree quit drinking cold turkey, but this time at her therapist's urging, she started attending women's recovery meetings. "My therapist kept telling me, 'I understand you're doing good, but willpower will fizzle out. You really need community.'"

She remembers being a fly on a wall for the first few meetings. "I finally shared, and I remember I was like a deer in headlights. I didn't know what to say. All I knew is that I'd found my people."

Other women shared similar hopes and fears, and it offered Desiree the validation and acceptance she'd been looking for. "I didn't feel alone anymore. And that was the puzzle piece. Community."

Facebook post from May 2019:

> *I went to a play date the other day at someone's house. Almost the moment I stepped through the front door, the mom giggled, "Mimosa time!" and my body froze up.*
>
> *I wasn't prepared for this.*
>
> *Most times, when I'm heading to a social gathering, I have time to prepare. I mentally prepare, I physically prepare (I always bring an alcohol-free drink with me), I emotionally prepare.*

I think about what I will say when someone asks why I'm not drinking. I think about how deep I want to get in the conversation—because some days I'm ready to go there, and other days I want to talk about anything BUT that.

Today, because I was so caught off guard, I almost said "Yes" and thought about just pretending to sip it. But I said, "Not right now, I'm good, thank you," and the conversation veered to something else.

But it came up again about 15 minutes later. And again another 15 minutes later. And I was practically banging my head against the wall mentally thinking, "Why don't I just tell her I don't drink?"

But I didn't. I was afraid she would think I wasn't fun. I was afraid she wouldn't want to have more play dates with me.

I read a meme yesterday that said, "I determine my kids play dates by which mom I want to drink wine with."

Being alcohol free can truly feel ostracizing. And it's strange to think that alcohol is the only drug that we have to explain NOT using.

Time to change the narrative. Alcohol free is a choice that should not require an explanation, embarrassment or fear of condemnation.

I'd written that piece seventeen months into my sobriety. I included a picture of me holding a letter board up that said, "Alcohol is the only drug we need to explain not using." The post went viral to millions and was shared on Facebook 125,000 times. It got picked up by the *Today Show*, Bored Panda, and Upworthy, to name a few. I even expanded on the piece for a byline in the *Washington Post*.

It's no secret why this piece resonated with so many people. In the comments you can hear so much pain, as many described how hard it is to make friends sober, how isolating it feels to be the only sober person in the room, and how awful it can be to see friends slowly (and quickly) stop calling and texting now that you're no longer Buzzed Betty, the party girl.

MAKING, KEEPING, AND LOSING FRIENDS

When people ask me if my friendships changed in sobriety, I assure them that yes, they changed forever. I did lose some friends when I quit drinking, and I also ended some friendships of my own accord too. And thank goodness.

In Laura McKowen's book, *We Are the Luckiest*, she says, "Drinking gave me the illusion of connection, though, so when I was drinking with people . . . I felt like we were getting closer. I felt like alcohol allowed us to break down barriers, to slide closer to our truer selves and to each other, closer than we could ever get without it. But when the buzz wore off, the separateness returned, and often it was intensely magnified."[1]

It doesn't take much time sober to realize that friendships built around heavy drinking are toxic. Some are downright dangerous. I dearly love many of my former drinking buddies, but in my path to wellness, I quickly realized I would need to make some tough decisions about how I spent my time and with whom—especially in that first year. I had to unfollow many of these friends on social media to avoid feeling that twinge of jealousy at seeing them out and about, partying it up at events where

I no longer felt comfortable. But I took solace in knowing this was the right journey for me. I was building trust and forming priceless memories with my children, and my body was healing.

It wasn't all doom and gloom. Many of my friends were supportive or at least indifferent toward my newly announced sobriety. As I spent time with these friends, I started to realize they weren't big drinkers and probably never had been. Had I projected my own obsession with alcohol on everyone else? It reminded me of the realization I'd had on our Mexico trip, when I was stunned that everyone wasn't there to get drunk. I saw now that many of my friends could have one or two and go home without sneaking in pours or shots or begging to go out for one last night cap.

An initial loneliness often comes when you first quit drinking. As Laura continues,

> "When I stopped drinking . . . I felt a loneliness like never before. There is a literal aspect to this: you left the proverbial island. All your friends live there, in that place, and you are actually going off into the unknown, away from the people and places and things that used to comfort you and catch you. But there's also the visceral aspect. Even if the connection was artificial . . . now that connection is gone. So even when I was with people, I had no idea how to connect to them. I would have never considered most of my relationships to be based on drinking, but when I started to get sober, I realized that most of them . . . were. Even the ones that weren't took time to recalibrate."[2]

This is one good reason the connections that come with a program, such as AA or rehab, are so critical in early sobriety. You are immediately introduced to others facing similar battles and interested in forging new relationships with people like you. You're all vulnerable and feeling abandoned by the inhabitants of your former island and are searching for others to fill that new void. But the many of us who don't feel drawn to a program, are newly sober curious, or just sick of the alcohol-obsessed culture we live in and want to break free of that narrative—we can feel left out in the cold. Are we destined to go this journey alone? Does anyone understand this middle gray area? The one that sits somewhere between never drinking and sneaking vodka throughout the day? Because that feels damn lonely too.

Friendships in motherhood are hard in general. Mothers don't have the privilege of free time, so finding ways to cultivate relationships with other moms often falls by the wayside or is based on the convenient match up according to kids' schooling or extracurriculars, which sometimes works out great but other times feel forced and superficial.

Amy Weatherly and Jess Johnston said it best in their book, *I'll Be There (But I'll Be Wearing Sweatpants)*: "Finding new people is exhausting. I mean, they're great, but it takes so long to break them in. They have to learn your quirks and your nuances and inside jokes, and you have to learn theirs, and it's just too much."[3]

I remember trying to build friendships years ago, before I was married or had children, by forming a book club with some other women I worked with. Everyone seemed enthusiastic about the idea, and I thought, "Alrighty, I'm going to make friends with these women and I'll invite them all over and we'll connect and it will be amazing." The Evite was out—six RSVPs! The appetizers were ready. I left work early that day to put the finishing touches on my picture-perfect first book club meeting. Here's the punch line: every single woman I'd invited stood me up that evening. One had the courtesy to text me and mention everyone seemed to be working late, but I will spare you the amount of ugly tears I shed that evening wondering why I'd even bothered.

According to a study published in the *Journal of Social and Personal Relationships*, it takes forty to sixty hours to form a casual friendship with someone and more than two hundred hours to form a close or best friend.[4] To which I say, "No wonder my social calendar is so bleak!" I'm lucky if I get an hour of time to spend with John each week, never mind with anyone else, especially now that I work from home full time. Who has time to develop friendships when I can't even get my kids to school or soccer practice on time? An hour for coffee with a friend feels like a luxury completely out of reach.

For years, I wandered through this makeshift friendship purgatory where connections felt superficial and fragile. Nurturing relationships seemed endless and impossible. Does she like me? Will they invite me? These questions weighed me down, and social media magnified the issue by showing me when and where my friend groups were hanging out without me—in real time. I can't say for certain now why my friends seemed to be distancing themselves from me, but at the time I blamed it on my sobriety.

And yet, I was extremely lucky because I found some incredible mom friends early in motherhood through my writing community. Our passions for writing and motherhood soon led to real-life friendships with women all over the country who I could cry, laugh, and share with, without judgment. They were my confidantes in my first year of recovery and became my biggest cheerleaders when I went public. But only one of them—my friend Jodie Utter—was sober; the rest drank.

Before I went public with my sobriety, I didn't know anyone who didn't drink, let alone anyone in recovery. When people join AA, they have an instant introduction to others in their shoes, but since that wasn't my path . . . where would I find other sober connections?

Believe it or not, as soon as I started writing about my sobriety, I began to connect with other people who also wrote about their sobriety on social media. That was how I found perhaps the most uplifting, safe, and motivating place on the internet: sober Instagram. The sober Instagram community is so full of energy, it feels how I assume a Katy Perry concert must feel. Through positive memes, quotes, and inspiring stories of people who have changed their lives through recovery, this space offers tremendous support to those who join in. I've found other women there, including moms, who come from all different paths and programs but who are all genuinely committed to sober living.

For the first time, I didn't feel like an outlier but a part of the majority. My Instagram feed was 90 percent sober related, 9 percent inspiration, and 1 percent secret celebrity crushes like Ryan Reynolds and Blake Lively. I felt embraced and accepted for my sober lifestyle in a way I never knew possible, and I only wished I'd uncovered this treasure trove sooner.

Then in March 2020, the pandemic hit. Schools were shut down overnight. The world felt like it was crumbling before our eyes. The media showed us images of overcrowded hospitals and people quarantined in their apartments in Italy singing to each other on balconies.

While I wasn't in a recovery program, I could hear the sheer terror in my feed from friends who no longer had a program or meetings to attend. It seemed like people were dropping like flies as I started reading posts about spikes in overdoses, falling off the wagon, and fear of the unknown. The mothers in our community felt especially unsettled. We all Googled "distance learning" and "home activities" while the world told us it was unsafe to leave our houses.

SOBER MOM SQUAD

My Instagram friend Emily Paulson posted a message asking if anyone was interested in partnering to serve the sober mom community with weekly Zoom calls just for mothers exploring an alcohol-free lifestyle, and I instinctively reached out with a big "Yes." While I was more than two years sober, the anxiety and paranoia brought on by so much change so quickly left me feeling vulnerable to relapse, and I needed something positive to immerse myself in.

With the support of several other Instagram mom friends, Emily led the charge on a free weekly virtual meeting that we called the Sober Mom Squad. I can't remember how many women joined our first meeting, maybe a couple dozen, but soon we had forty to fifty women on these calls, connecting week after week to share and connect.

This was the first kind of meeting I'd ever attended in my sobriety, and I felt completely out of my element. It was one thing to write my heart out on the computer, but to see a screen of fifty women and look them in the eye and tell them I feel like I'm failing as a mom was a vulnerability like nothing I'd ever known. Even more, these women would share their hard truths right back. We would laugh, we would cry, we would cheer each other on, and we would connect with each other on a level our own partners and children couldn't.

At two years sober, I was one of the old timers. Many of the women on our calls were days or weeks into their recovery. Tears flowed as we bared our souls and found common ground in the fear and uncertainty that gripped us in that time of isolation and anxiety.

Johann Hari famously said that the opposite of addiction is connection, and rat experiments in the 1970s and 1980s concluded that rats are more inclined to drink drug-laced water when they are alone and unstimulated, versus when caged with other rats where they have social connections.[5]

The irony in motherhood, however, is mothers are anything but unstimulated. We are bombarded by stimulation. It's crushing and constant, occurring at all hours of the day and night, often leaving us sleep deprived and drained. If anything, I would argue moms are overstimulated with human connection, and many of us would kill for a few moments of peace and quiet each day.

One of the attractions of alcohol is its ability to soften the noise and stimulation. We can't turn the volume down on our kids, nor can we wear noise-canceling headphones all day. But a few glasses of wine a night? That does the trick. So when I go back to Johann Hari's theory on connection, I think the key is, *what kind of connection?* I think social connection is the ticket to relief here, a connection to friends or others with similar interests or goals.

Laura McKowen takes it another step. She speaks about intimacy, referring to it as "a kind compassionate witness" to our deepest thoughts and feelings. I don't know about you, but most of my friendships barely scratched the surface of this type of intimacy. Even romantic relationships in my life always held a certain element of secret keeping. Who wants to know about my demons, after all? What a great way to scare someone off.

This is why group therapy and meetings feel like such game changers. Unlike individual therapy, group therapy fosters a give-and-take environment, where you're encouraged to openly communicate your struggles, which then generates feedback and support from other participants. You not only feel relief at verbalizing what's in your head and heart, but you also feel a spirit of service through uplifting the other group members. Group therapy and meetings help us know we are not alone and that others share similar concerns or struggles. Psychiatrist Dr. Irvin David Yalom, a group therapy expert, refers to this as the principle of "universality."[6] There are few things more validating than hearing someone else share your same fears, your same mistakes, and your same patterns of behavior. Is there anything more relieving than hearing your own story in someone else's words? "Same, friend, same," you think to yourself as you nod in accordance, because you've been there too.

While the Sober Mom Squad was neither therapy nor a recovery program like AA, it was a soft place to land, so to speak. And there was an easiness and comfort in that it felt less "official," more "come as you are." And there were no expectations: do or don't share, even have your video off if you don't want to be seen.

When I spoke with Emily Paulson, she shared what called her to start the group. "I feel like this is something that we needed all along. We have people who've had rock bottom stories and people who are sober curious. But it was important to find and support this middle ground, the people doing the private 'Am I am alcoholic?' Google searches while in public pretending they're fine. [On top of that is feeling the] added pressure of being a mom. Just to have a place they could go and speak without fear of judgement felt more important than ever."

It wasn't until I started attending and leading Sober Mom Squad meetings that I began to find firm footing in the process of my healing. Through hearing other women's stories and how they found success or where they fell flat, I started to connect back to my own why and how, challenging my past convictions about who I am and how I got here. I listened to what worked for some, and I took mental notes. I heard about triggers and relapse and started to connect my own dots around what I needed to do in my life to get stronger, be more resilient. And of course, I heard horror stories. Stories of losing everything, families turning their backs, children who stopped talking to their mothers. DUIs, accidents, and health nightmares. No one had a success story from their drinking. Not a single one of us. No one in our circle had found a way to successfully moderate. Alcohol took and took and took some more—so many of the women in these meetings were fighting to stay alive.

Sometimes, when I look at the fifty faces in Brady Bunch–style boxes filling the screen in front of me, I choke up, thinking how proud I am to be part of this group of women. No one is forcing them to be there. They're all there because they want more for themselves, for their families, for their futures. How brave these women are to show up, sometimes multiple times a day. How beautiful it is to hear other mothers letting down their guards and feeling safe to say the hard, ugly truths that we often feel we have to hide in the real world.

Taylor Swift wrote a song about people who are struggling with hidden pain, such as addiction, called "this is me trying" on her album *Folklore*. She said it was about the work people put in when they're trying to recover, which often is unseen and unnoticed. One meeting I played the song for the women, and I silently wept as Taylor's words flowed through the computer speakers.

After the song played, I looked at the women on the screen and I told them that I see them. I see each of them trying and that I know it's hard, and I know many people in their lives don't understand or don't care or don't even see. But I see them. I see them trying.

Group therapy, AA meetings, and recovery circles have been around for a long time. Once the pandemic hit, their sudden changeover to virtual meetings had a huge positive impact on mothers seeking support. Suddenly, mothers could log in with their phones. They didn't need someone to watch the kids or to even bring the kids with them to a meeting. It mitigated one of the biggest concerns I'd had when I was first in recovery, when I wasn't yet ready to explain to my husband that I needed his help so I could go to a meeting called (gulp!) Alcoholics Anonymous. I knew other women would feel as I had, that it was selfish to take time for myself for almost anything, never mind to openly admit to being an alcoholic who needs to go to meetings. But virtual meetings, held at convenient times, were a way to test the waters, find community, feel less guilty. They were a game-changing boon to mothers entering or in recovery.

Sober Mom Squad was literally born out of this opportunity. Other virtual groups rose at that time as well, and more traditional groups such as AA made the transition online, too.

While the pandemic disrupted so much of our life, the "Zoomi-fication" (not a word but fun to say out loud) of recovery meetings might go down as the greatest disruptor of all, and for the better.

"To be able to go on a Zoom call, be completely anonymous, have your video off, never say a word, and just listen and hear stories that might resonate with you?" said Paulson. "You can put your earbuds on and have your kids around and it doesn't matter. I think that's been such a barrier and a need that wasn't fulfilled for a long time."

PRIORITIZING CONNECTION

The other day I was picking my dog up from the groomer, and I bumped into one of the moms from my son's school. We had hung out a number of times, and I even attended her daughter's birthday a few months earlier. She was one of those people that I seemed to run into constantly, and I thought to myself, "We should be friends. Why aren't we friends?" And of course, the answer is we're both shuffling between full-time jobs and raising kids, nurturing our marriages, and still trying to squeeze in a run or a yoga class. Making time for friendship almost feels, well, selfish. Certainly unproductive. Therefore not a priority.

In her podcast, *We Can Do Hard Things*, Glennon Doyle spoke to this predicament. "It's like the capitalistic idea . . . the most immediate goal is production. *What am I making?* Friendship . . . is such a wild resistance to capitalistic productivity addiction. You're sitting with your friend and you're like, 'What freaking good is this hour?' It's such a wild thing to commit yourself to because it feels like there's nothing to show for it afterwards."[7]

And yet, by definition, friendship is considered a stable, positive, reciprocal relationship that lifts our happiness levels and feels satisfying. As Glennon's sister, Amanda, the unofficial researcher for the podcast, says, "Science says satisfaction with relationships is the best predictor of health at eighty years old." So while we live in a productivity-obsessed society, and friendship is not defined as "productive," it does contribute to a happy, healthy life, which in my opinion is a pretty important goal.

I love the friendships that have us leaving the coffee shop with smiles plastered across our faces and feeling like our cup's been filled. What's better than picking right back up where you left off with a friend you haven't seen in a while and having a gab fest? But it comes with a price: the sneaky beast of guilt always looms nearby. As if I should be spending time with family or doing something "important" instead. But *only* spending time with family can be draining, leaving me feeling empty.

It breaks my heart that mommy guilt has followed me from my drinking even into sobriety. According to *A Sober Moms Guide to Recovery*, "Guilt is the constant companion of the alcoholic or addict, maybe even more so for a mom. Every mother feels guilt about her parenting from time to time. That's doubly true for women who have created drama and caused distress for their children by drinking or using—possibly inflicting psychological damage."[8]

Guilt and shame are common feelings for those of us in recovery for substance use disorder or addiction. They have been constant companions. And when we quit drinking or using, these habitual feelings often remain, even when we've made great strides into growing and improving our lives. Those are two emotions I've spent years in therapy trying to overcome.

I remember when my therapist once asked me, "You say you've forgiven your dad for his addiction and the pain it caused you, so why can't you forgive yourself?"

We moms are our own harshest critics. We expect so much and we aren't willing to accept anything less than perfect. During most of my day I was always on, like the Energizer Bunny. Wine gave me permission to pause. Only when I was numbing out was I able to give myself permission not to be achieving or be productive.

Through sobriety and therapy, I've learned how to allow myself time to take a breath without the assistance of a mind-altering substance. But letting go of the guilt or shame that follows takes even more work, grace, and self-compassion.

And do you know what else takes work? Yep, nurturing friendships. As an introvert, it feels a heck of a lot easier to say, "Maybe another time." But when I do say yes, when I do take a deep breath and get in the car and meet a girlfriend for a coffee date, I always come away feeling more fulfilled. And it doesn't take scientific evidence for me to see that I'm a happier, healthier person for making that time.

LIGHTEN YOUR LOAD

♦ Find a group to help you connect with others. Whether it's through a formal recovery program or not, there are so many groups related to sobriety, motherhood, or both. The best part is that the groups do the scheduling; your only job is to show up! Of course, I recommend Sober Mom Squad because I lead meetings there every week, but a simple Google search will help you find many groups compatible with your own needs. For example, look up "AA meetings near me," or if you want to try something outside of AA, look up "10 alternatives to Alcoholics Anonymous."

- According to the book *I'll Be There (But I'll Be Wearing Sweat Pants)*, "Step one is admitting you need friends. Step two is getting out into the world where you can find them." Authors Amy Weatherly and Jess Johnston recommend joining a gym, volunteering at school, finding a bible study class, or inviting coworkers out for lunch.[9]

- Commit yourself to a goal and be realistic. I once set a goal of one coffee date a week, and that blew up in my face fast, simply because it seemed like every date scheduled had to be rescheduled two or three times. Because, well, #momlife. I think a solid commitment to one date with a friend a month (kids' playdates count—win/win!) is an awesome place to start.

- Your sobriety does not mean you have to start from scratch in your friendships. Some of these friendships will flourish in your sobriety—you'll be surprised! When you start spending time with friends under a new sober mindset, you'll be fascinated with how friendships might shift for the better. Reframe your thoughts to spend less time thinking about the friends who suddenly disappeared when you mentioned your new interest in sober living, and instead look at the friends who leaned in.

- I asked my social media followers how they find and nurture sober friendships and got a few gems I want to share: Shanin says, "Don't be afraid, reach out. The people meant for you will stay. Don't worry about the ones that fall away. They simply weren't for you." Bridget says: "Just show up. Have fun, be there, and show it." Joanna wisely states: "Host the event, invite the people. Repeat ad nauseam until you find your core." And my number one fan, Carla (disclaimer, she's also my mom) shared: "Everything we do touches others, even if we feel insignificant. A compliment, text, or kind gesture can stay with a person long after. You often never know how the little things you do affect others for quite a long time."

9 | THE GOOD NEWS . . . AND IT'S GREAT NEWS, ACTUALLY

KRISTIN'S STORY

Kristin, thirty-eight, got in touch with me over Instagram to say she'd followed me for years but really needed help now. While hers wasn't the first message like this I'd received, something in her message especially resonated with me. I experienced a déjà vu of emotions from my early days in sobriety.

Fear. Shame. Desperation.

I knew that mix of feelings all too well.

I told Kristin to hop on a Sober Mom Squad meeting, and she did that same day. That was 569 days ago, she proudly reminded me when we reconnected over the phone recently.

Kristin grew up around alcohol and started drinking as early as eighth grade. While she partied in high school and college like many others, she thrived at school and went on to become a nurse. Married and expecting her first child by age twenty-six, Kristin soon realized the heartbreak of her spouse's addiction to drugs and alcohol. Even during that experience and dealing with their subsequent divorce, she never saw her own drinking as a problem. "I didn't drink every day, and I thought I had it under control."

Kristin says her drinking picked up a lot after the divorce. Parenting was lonely, and drinking helped pass the time. Eventually she started dating again and met someone really special, but her drinking was getting out of control with regular blackouts, making plans around alcohol, and doing embarrassing things. "My kids were starting to say things like, 'Mom, you're drinking again?' And I knew I was going to lose [my boyfriend] too."

After a particularly mortifying camping trip where she got blackout drunk in front of all their friends, Kristin got sick and tired of her own crap, and that's when she reached out to me. Kristin's entire life changed with her sobriety, starting with rebuilding her relationships with her kids and her partner.

"The first three months were awful," she remembers. "I questioned myself a lot. I wondered if this was necessary—do I really need to stop?"

One night her kids called her, crying uncontrollably. They told her that their biological dad was lying on the floor unresponsive and they didn't know how to handle it. In the past, Kristin would be drinking by this time and in no shape to drive. But Kristin was stone-cold sober and ready to jump in the car, fully able both to drive and talk her kids through what to do. "It was an ah-ha moment that this is what I want. I'm on the right path."

Shortly after Kristin hit ninety days sober, her boyfriend proposed, and they've since gotten married. "I never imagined having a wedding sober! I had the absolutely best time." And recently she got a puppy. "It's a totally different life, a life I never imagined." And it's an alternate reality to where she might be now if she were still drinking.

Excerpt from my Blog

September 22, 2020

   My favorite moments in parenting were never the wine-soaked half memories of what may or may not have happened at the birthday party, the playdate, or the mimosa-fueled brunch.

   I do not look back on any of the hard times, when I struggled with PPD and anxiety and couldn't sleep more than a few hours at a time, and wished I'd drunk more.

   I can never go back and relive some of my babies' firsts: first steps, first words, first time they blew me a kiss—and experience them sober. Feel the natural joy and euphoria of those precious moments without a few glasses of wine dulling my senses.

   Nor will I miss the frustrations, the inner desperation of trying to merge my old independent self to this new one, to merge my old life with my unrecognizably exhausting mom existence. I certainly don't wonder for even a second if more alcohol might have helped.

   Despite all the credit we give alcohol for helping us 'survive' parenting, I can truly look back and appreciate 0% of the role it played in my motherhood. You will never hear me wish I drank more to survive the challenges of parenting. Because, in truth, drinking only took away from my ability to cope.

   And for all the time, money, and energy I spent convincing myself that 'mommy needs wine' to appreciate the milestones, I am left with fuzzier memories and ample regrets. And as mothers we deserve so much more than that. So do our children.

"Stone cold sober needs a re-brand," says Catherine Gray in *The Unexpected Joy of Being Sober*. "It should be called 'sunshine-warm sober' instead. Because that's what it feels like. The loveliness of daylight, clarity, and authentic social connection."[1]

It seems terribly ill-fitting to end my book, as many quit-lit books do, at the start of my sobriety. After all, isn't this really just the beginning? The beauty of sobriety is the metamorphosis into the butterfly, and yet you got to hear me ramble on and on about my caterpillar days.

While this is not even close to the end of my story, it is the end of this story. And, as in the end of so many stories where the person finally lets go of a toxic relationship, this is one of hope and encouragement. Good things happen when we put down the bottle. There *is* light at the end of the hangover. The beautiful part about sobriety is that you get your life back. My story and the stories of other mothers will help women turn the tables before it's too late, before the addiction overtakes one of the greatest gifts of our existence: being a mom.

I hate thinking about how much time I've wasted. It's easy to get lost in that dialogue. Because looking back, I want to kick myself.

What was I waiting for?

So much time lost. So many blackouts or missed moments. So much anxiety, risk, struggle, and regret. I have to remind myself over and over again that I didn't know what I didn't know.

I thought quitting meant the end of all things good. I believed quitting was the punishment.

You can't handle your alcohol? Go sit at the kids' table for the rest of your life and you can gaze at us "responsible drinkers" from afar. Go sit in church-basement meetings and confess your struggles to your kind only; the rest of us don't want to hear it. Go live a life of deprivation, anonymity, and social incarceration.

But sobriety wasn't the punishment.

Sobriety was the reward.

Addiction was the punishment. Alcohol was the toxic partner, the crawl through hell, the parasite lodged in my body. And the irony of it all? I thought it was doing me favors. Subconsciously I thought I needed it. I couldn't imagine evenings, parties, or celebrations without it, when in fact the only thing alcohol has ever given me was a severe, unbearable hangover. Otherwise it took, took, took.

Sobriety was my path home. It was the only way I could connect back to myself, the little Celeste who started losing herself the moment she decided what other people thought of her was more important than how she felt about herself. The person who got so lost in the shuffle of drinking she didn't even know who she was anymore.

In my sobriety I realized I've been trying to hide from those questions ever since I started counting my calories or binging and purging hours of my day during my teen years. It was only when I finally stopped hiding from everything that I could begin nurturing the most important relationship of my life: the one with myself.

Sobriety takes us to that place to which many of us aspire: building awareness and appreciation for the present. Think about how many people spend their lives in therapy or do meditation practices, read books by spiritual thinkers, or attend religious/spiritual services in order to reconnect with their inner divine souls.

Sobriety gets us there. Sometimes it's an unpredictable road or at least starts with a steep drop. Some paths are windy or broken, long or painful, but this road inevitably evens out. Before long, you start to look up and look around and you see the colors, you smell the fresh air. You realize this path was the prize all along. No one told us it would be this rewarding.

There's an important distinction I need to make here between literal sobriety and emotional sobriety. Sobriety can be defined simply as abstinence from drinking or using other substances, but what I'm referring to in the reward is what comes with emotional sobriety.

When I first started writing about my recovery publicly, someone called me a "dry drunk" on social media and I had no idea what they meant. After an intense Google search, I learned that a dry drunk is considered someone who has cut out alcohol but hasn't done "the work." While this particular person was referring to the work of the 12-step program in AA, I'd prefer to think that the work refers to anything you do to achieve emotional sobriety. (I recognize that some hard-lined AA-ers would argue against this, but as you know, I believe there are numerous alternatives to AA.)

Emotional sobriety is learning to regulate your emotions to endure the kind of feelings that previously triggered your drinking. People can achieve this through all sorts of self-work and healing, therapy, and practice. There isn't just one answer.

You can spend your life sober from alcohol, but if you're white knuckling every day of your life, you need to start working on how to set down that lead backpack if you want to ever feel the true satisfaction of a sober life. We hear a lot about people who quit drinking but go on to replace that addiction with deep-seated rage or verbal/physical abuse of others. Cross-addictions are common, and many can transition from alcohol to addictions involving work, sex, gaming, or just about anything else you can think of.

That's not the sobriety I'm talking about. That's just exchanging one problem, one crutch, for another. Emotional sobriety can take years to achieve. Veronica Valli, author, recovery coach, and psychotherapist, compares early sobriety to being an emotion-filled teenager. We have to learn new skills for navigating emotions that we previously numbed out or pushed aside. It takes time and work to feel comfortable in our own skin.

Valli explains in her book, *Soberful*, that we employ four skills in achieving emotional sobriety: setting boundaries, balancing needs, dealing with resentments, and changing our limiting beliefs. And while Valli argues emotional sobriety is a destination—"reaching a place where you can live in the present without fear or discomfort,"[2] I would also add these are skills that we can continue to build and grow on to enhance the rest of our lives.

"The work of emotional sobriety lasts our lifetime. . . . We are all 'becoming' and we will never really stop," Valli says.[3]

I don't think that I was a dry drunk when that person commented on my post. While I didn't go to AA, I'd already started doing the work to achieve emotional sobriety. I may not have reached my destination of total confidence at the time (not even close!), but I was strong enough not to let an ugly comment break my stride. And I think that says something.

WHO CARES?

It occurred to me recently that all the skeletons in my closet are loud and proud on the internet for the world to see. My exes, friends from childhood, and everyone in between can pop on to my social media pages and learn anything and everything about me. Including the secrets I kept bottled up for years.

After a moment of letting that sink in, I realized, who cares?

It reminds me of a quote that said, "Using my past to hurt me is like trying to rob my old house. I don't live there anymore. That's not my stuff."[4]

When my ego stopped trying so hard to control the narrative, I was able to let a lot of these fears slide. Not all of them, of course. But enough that I can look at the secrets I've uncovered and made public through my writing over the years, and now through this book, and know that what others think about me is irrelevant.

Fear of how people would react to my sobriety weighed on me heavily for a long time; for a long time it felt like an obsession. What if people think of me as an alcoholic?

Who cares?

While social media has its significant problems, I also believe it's done recovery and sobriety a huge service. A decade or two ago, someone's drinking struggles would induce whispers. It would arouse gossip and hearsay, judgment, and shame. The more people speak publicly (and let's face it, social media gives everyone a platform) about topics like gray-area drinking, addiction, and mental health, the more we are collectively saying, who cares? To the ugly stigmas of generations past:

Alcohol addiction means the end.

Sobriety is boring.

An addict is a derelict.

It's time to call BS. Look around today and see that some of the most incredible and inspiring people in entertainment and media are sober and proud. Blake Lively, Jennifer Lopez, Robert Downey Jr., and Jennifer Hudson for starters. Glennon Doyle, Brené Brown, Dax Shepard, and 50 Cent, if you want to keep making lists. I could talk about this all day.

There are so many reasons people choose not to drink alcohol. Some of these people hit rock bottom in the public eye, others never liked alcohol to begin with, and still others abstain because it's deeply hurt or killed their loved ones. Their reasons for abstaining are across the board. Someday I hope we can collectively reach a place where, when someone—be it a celebrity, neighbor, coworker, or friend—says they don't drink, the common response is neutrality. Indifference. And yes, "Who cares?" (in the most loving of ways).

When someone says no to a drink, it doesn't say anything about that person except that they don't want a drink. And I say, "Good for them!"

THE NEXT CHAPTER

When my dad died a few years ago, I was still relatively new to my sober lifestyle. I was glad he got to see me sober before he passed, as I know watching me stumble on the same bumps that tripped him up must have hit him hard.

My dad spent his life chasing the illusive aspects of alcohol, always just one sip away from satisfaction. His life, and his family's, would always be shadowed by the darkness of addiction. Through the rehabs, the trips to ER, the secrets, and the lies, alcohol gave back nothing.

The day he died, I sat next to him on the hospital bed as his breathing slowed, his eyes softened. I felt sad and helpless, nauseous with knowing this moment was so fleeting. But there was a peacefulness in the air too.

My mom talked to him quietly, whispering memories of happier times. The sun flickered through the windows between cloud covering, and the air outside was damp from light rainfall. My mom spoke of trips together, family moments, funny stories. My aunt sat close and silently rubbed my dad's tired, swollen feet, nodding to my mom's stories and sometimes laughing or stopping my mom's story to ask a question.

My dad struggled his whole life to find solid footing. He spent the first half of his life drowning himself in alcohol and the second half trying to physically stop an addiction that now had more power over him than his love for his family, or even his will to live.

I wonder if, once my dad's addiction gripped him for good, he ever felt the sweet satisfaction of anything ever again. Maybe now, in this next space, he can finally reach some peace. Maybe in death he can finally be present—whatever that looks like. Because I don't know what comes after this life, but anyone who's battled addiction has already been to hell and back. It would be great if the afterlife offers some well-needed closure.

And of course, there was a bittersweet sensation running through me as I held his hand for those final breaths. Because with the sadness I also felt pride. Dad, I will not let alcohol take me down. Your struggle was not in vain. I will break this generational curse, and your grandchildren will be stronger for it. I know you felt like you lost the battle, but I can only end the cycle because of you.

And after my dad's final breaths, after the melodic beep of the heart monitor settled into a slow, despondent buzz, after the nurse came in and confirmed what we already knew, after my mom, my aunt, and I stopped crying and hugging, finally gathering our things to leave, I took one last look at my dad.

Dad, this isn't the end. This is only the next chapter of our epic comeback story. Your journey continues through everything you've shown and taught me, and I will carry your heart with me in what I do next. Your suffering was not in vain; you infused a strength in me that never would have otherwise existed. Addiction is not your legacy. Your legacy is what happens next. And dad? Wait till you see what happens next.

LIGHTEN YOUR LOAD

- The most impactful way to quit drinking *and* stay sober is through doing the work. Whether your journey is through AA or an alternative program or group, I encourage you to find a support system that fits your beliefs, personality, and motivators. AA's twelve steps is the most well-known "work" out there and I have many friends who swear by the steps. But if you're seeking another way, you don't identify as an "alcoholic," or you're looking less for a program than for a more individualistic way to sustain sobriety, there are plenty of options to choose from. *Quit Like a Woman*, by Holly Whitaker, details a long-term recovery process you can follow, and there are many other online support programs and meetings, such as She Recovers, Join Monument, SMART Recovery, The Luckiest Club, and The Temper.

- While it's easy to get swept up in the "quitting drinking" aspect of recovery, getting at the core reason behind how we got there is essential to staying sober. Often drinking or drug use is rooted in coping mechanisms we'd used when confronted with childhood trauma, anxiety, or other mental health struggles. Consider doing some psychological work—with a professional if possible—to dig at the story behind the drinking. It's important to distinguish therapy from recovery programs, which each serve different, cohesive purposes.

♦ Just as important as finding a long-term solution is acknowledging and addressing the "why" of our present-day struggles. The mental load of motherhood, anxiety or depression, stress at work, and the overwhelming culture of busyness all play into severe feelings of burnout. These must be addressed here and now so we don't fall back on old patterns of numbing.

♦ I asked my social media followers what their favorite parts of long-term sobriety included. Courtney said, "My now husband got sober, then 2 years later, we got married! Now, I couldn't imagine life without him." Ted wrote, "Because I got sober, I ended up not losing my wife and kids." Mary wrote, "I stopped trying to escape motherhood and actually started to enjoy it." Sharona: "I was able to help my BFF's husband and daughter care for her when she was terminal." Nancy: "I found myself. I found out who I really am without alcohol and I am quite amazing. And happy." I have never heard a story of long-term sobriety that didn't serve as a beautiful, important gift for someone and their family.

♦ It's time to end the stigma around sobriety! There is absolutely nothing to be ashamed of in our sober journeys. The more people who speak up and talk openly about

addiction, recovery, and sobriety, the more people struggling will feel safe to seek help, open up, or simply recognize the problem. I imagine a future where binge drinking
isn't an expected part of the college experience, where
friends meeting up for drinks automatically includes both
alcoholic and nonalcoholic options, and where a mother
struggling elicits genuine concern and offers of support
instead of jokes about wine being the solution to anything that ails her. What an inclusive, supportive, glorious
world that would be.

RESOURCE LIBRARY

BOOKS

This Naked Mind, Annie Grace
We Are the Luckiest, Laura McKowen
Not Drinking Tonight, Amanda White
Quit Like a Woman, Holly Whitaker
Hey Hun, Emily Paulson
Drink, Ann Dowsett Johnston
The Unexpected Joy of Being Sober, Catherine Gray
Dopamine Nation, Anna Lembke
Fed Up, Gemma Hartley
Fair Play, Eve Rodsky
Blackout, Sarah Heppola

PODCASTS

Sober Powered
We Can Do Hard Things
Soberful, Veronica Valli and Chip Somers
Sober Black Girls Club Podcast
In Recovery with Dr. Nzinga Harrison
The Sober Gay Podcast
Rich Roll Podcast

COMMUNITIES

Sober Mom Squad
We Are the Luckiest
Alcoholics Anonymous
Sober Sis
SMART Recovery
This Naked Mind Group
Sober Black Girls Club
She Recovers
Women for Sobriety
Gays and Lesbians in Alcoholics Anonymous (GaL-AA)

INSPIRATIONAL INSTAGRAM PAGES TO FOLLOW

@sobergirlsociety
@thesobersenorita
@soberbrowngirls
@pattersonperspective
@sobrietyactivist
@tawnymlara
@yoursoberpal
@1000hoursdry
@mybadassrecovery
@teedoodler
@therapyforwomen
@sobermomsquad

SOBER APPS

Sober Buddy
I Am Sober
The Alcohol Experiment
Sober Mom Squad
Reframe

ACKNOWLEDGMENTS

I'm sitting here in disbelief that I actually reached the part of the book-writing process where I get to acknowledge those who helped make this possible. This book has evolved along with my sober journey, and it would look very different if I'd written it a few years ago as I'd originally hoped. Between the pandemic, my personal growth, and life changes all around, much of what I needed to experience to make this book whole happened long after I thought I was ready to write it. I am reminded yet again of that Garth Brooks quote, "Some of God's greatest gifts are unanswered prayers."

To my agent, Chris Tomasino, who believed in me and my writing even before I did. You saw the vision for this book and was the one to nudge me to dream bigger. To my friends at Broadleaf Books who took a chance on a first-time author because they recognized the importance of this message. Lisa Kloskin, Sydney Miller, and Adrienne Ingrum . . . you made magic with my ramblings. You connected the dots. You helped me transform thousands of words into a complete picture, frame, and all. And the entire team who helped us get here: Erin Gibbons, Elle Rogers, Jana Nelson, Annette Hughes, and Olga Grlic for the gorgeous cover design.

To my friends in the recovery community who make me laugh, cry, and reflect daily. I don't want to do this journey without you.

My family has been my strongest supporter in all of this. Thank you to my husband and boys for cheering me on throughout this process. Thank you, Mom, for always being my shoulder to lean on when times got hard. To my brother and sister and my in-laws, you really are my dream team in everything I do. My dear mother-in-law, Sheila, passed away during the making of this book. Thank you, Sheila, for loving and accepting me just as I am. I see you every day in your grandchildren. B recently said he wants to be a birdwatcher, and I thought, *"Just like Grandma Sheila."*

And Dad? It wouldn't be much of an acknowledgment if I didn't include the greatest inspiration of all. I know you are somewhere out there watching me and giving a great big whistle and clap. This may be a book about moms, but it was inspired and born from my relationship with you, Dad. When I lift my eyes off the stressors, the triggers, or intrusive thoughts, I see you every day in the fluttering butterfly, the purposeful dragonfly, and the occasional rainbow. All I have to do is look up.

NOTES

CHAPTER 1

1 Megan Zander, "This Joke We Make About Wine-Drinking Moms Is Actually Really Screwed Up," Romper, July 11, 2017, https://www.romper.com/p/this-joke-we-make-about-wine-drinking-moms-is-actually-really-screwed-up-69087.

2 https://twitter.com/ramblinma?s=20.

3 "Alcohol and Cancer," Centers for Disease Control and Prevention, last modified January 31, 2022, https://www.cdc.gov/cancer/alcohol/index.htm.

4 "How Addictive Is Alcohol?" Washburn House, November 14, 2019, https://www.washburnhouse.com/addiction-recovery-blog/how-addictive-is-alcohol/.

5 tiadmin, "Mother's Little Helper at 50," Proto, September 22, 2013, http://protomag.com/articles/anniversary-valium-turns-50.

6 Taylor Prewitt, "Take Some Pills for Your Hysteria, Lady: America's Long History of Drugging Women Up," Vice, April 28, 2015, https://www.vice.com/en/article/gqmx9j/here-lady-take-some-pills-for-your-hysteria-253.

7 tiadmin, "Mother's Little Helper at 50."

8 Ann Dowsett Johnston, *Drink* (New York: Harper Wave, 2013), 67.

9 Holly Whitaker, *Quit Like a Woman* (New York: Random House, 2019), 59.

10 Dowsett Johnston, *Drink*, 66.

11 Nicola Carruthers, "Alcohol Ad Spend to Hit $6bn by 2023," The Spirits Business, May 24, 2021, https://www.thespiritsbusiness.com/2021/05/alcohol-ad-spend-to-hit-6bn-by-2023/.
12 Whitaker, *Quit Like a Woman*, 59.
13 Anne Helen Petersen, "The Subtle Look and Overwhelming Feel of Today's Misogyny," Culture Study, November 7, 2021, https://annehelen.substack.com/p/the-subtle-look-and-overwhelming.
14 Dowsett Johnston, *Drink*, 69.
15 Debra Fulghum Bruce, PhD, "Postpartum Depression," WebMD, August 23, 2021, https://www.webmd.com/depression/guide/postpartum-depression.
16 "Hangxiety: The Link Between Anxiety and Alcohol," Henry Ford Health, March 5, 2019, https://www.henryford.com/blog/2019/03/hangxiety-link-between-anxiety-alcohol.
17 Kristeen Churney, "Alcohol and Anxiety," Healthline, September 6, 2019, https://www.healthline.com/health/alcohol-and-anxiety#:~:text=Alcohol%20changes%20levels%20of%20serotonin,an%20entire%20day%20after%20drinking.
18 Amanda White, *Not Drinking Tonight* (New York: Hatchett, 2022), 1167, 170.

CHAPTER 2

1 Susan McQuillan, "Women and Eating Disorders," Psycom, May 28, 2021, https://www.psycom.net/women-eating-disorders/.
2 "Substance Use and Eating Disorders," National Eating Disorders, https://www.nationaleatingdisorders.org/substance-use-and-eating-disorders.

CHAPTER 3

1 Gemma Hartley, *Fed Up: Emotional Labor, Women, and the Way Forward* (New York: HarperOne, 2018), 9.
2 "The Mental Load of Motherhood," thedotcanada, 2021, https://www.thedotcanada.ca/blog-mental-health-ontario-canada/the-mental-load-of-motherhood.

3 Joseph Barberio, "This Comic Perfectly Explains the Mental Load Working Mothers Bear," Working Mother, November 2, 2018, https://www.workingmother.com/this-comic-perfectly-explains -mental-load-working-mothers-bear.

4 Hartley, *Fed Up*, 13.

5 Hartley, *Fed Up*, 5.

6 Rochelle Rodney, "Society Expects Black Single Mums To Fail. I Won't Be Written Off," HuffingtonPost, September 16, 2020, https://www.huffingtonpost.co.uk/entry/black-single-mums-suc cess_uk_5f60e80bc5b68d1b09c86aad.

7 Hartley, *Fed Up*, 54.

8 George Gao and Gretchen Livingston, "Working while Pregnant Is Much More Common Than It Used To Be," Pew Research Center, March 31, 2015, https://www.pewresearch.org/fact-tank /2015/03/31/working-while-pregnant-is-much-more-common -than-it-used-to-be/.

9 Marguerite Ward, "10 Countries That Show Just How Behind the US Is in Paid Parental Leave for New Mothers and Fathers," Insider, last modified May 5, 2020, https://www.businessinsider .com/countries-with-best-parental-leave-2016-8.

10 "At Some Point, Nearly Everyone Will Need To Take Time Away from Work to Deal with a Serious Personal or Family Health Con- dition, or To Bond with a New Child," National Partnership for Women and Families, 2022, https://www.nationalpartnership.org /our-work/economic-justice/paid-leave.html.

11 "Maternity Leave by Country," World Population Review, 2022, https://worldpopulationreview.com/country-rankings/maternity -leave-by-country.

12 Cheridan Christnacht and Briana Sullivan, "The Choices Work- ing Mothers Make," US Census Bureau, May 8, 2020, https:// www.census.gov/library/stories/2020/05/the-choices-working -mothers-make.html.

13 https://twitter.com/jasonmustian.

14 Misty L. Heggeness, Jason Fields, Yazmin A. García Trejo, and Anthony Schulzetenberg, "Moms, Work and the Pandemic," US

Census Bureau, March 3, 2021, https://www.census.gov/library /stories/2021/03/moms-work-and-the-pandemic.html.

15 Heggeness, Fields, García Trejo, and Schulzetenberg, "Moms, Work."

16 Anne Colaiacovo, "The Working Mother's Bill of Rights," PR Week, May 10, 2021, https://www.prweek.com/article/1715084 /working-mothers-bill-rights.

17 Beth Barry, "Dear Mothers: We Can't Keep Pretending This Is Working for Us," Revolution from Home, September 26, 2019, https://revolutionfromhome.com/2019/09/dear-mothers-we -cant-keep-pretending-this-is-working-for-us/.

18 Eve Rodsky, *Fair Play* (New York: G. P. Putnam's Sons, 2019), 34.

19 Celeste Yvonne, "I'm a Mom Who Self-Medicates, and It's Complicated," Scary Mommy, last modified July 2, 2020, https://www .scarymommy.com/mom-who-self-medicates-its-complicated/.

20 Sarah Lobello Pearson, "Can I Drink Alcohol with Antidepressants Like Zoloft?" GoodRx Health, May 25, 2021, https://www .goodrx.com/classes/ssris/can-i-drink-alcohol-while-taking-zoloft.

21 Dowsett Johnston, *Drink*, 128.

22 Olivia Remes, "Women Are Far More Anxious Than Men— Here's the Science," The Conversation, June 10, 2016, https:// theconversation.com/women-are-far-more-anxious-than-men -heres-the-science-60458.

23 http://www.gemmahartley.com/.

24 Gemma Hartley, interview with author, March 3, 2022.

25 Ginny Graves, "Why Alcohol Use Has Increased Among Women— And How It Has Affected Them," Health, March 19, 2019, https://www.health.com/condition/alcoholism/rethink-relation ship-to-alcohol.

26 Graves, "Why Alcohol."

27 Sasha Pezenik, "Alcohol Consumption Rising Sharply During Pandemic, Especially among Women," ABCNews, September 29, 2020, https://abcnews.go.com/US/alcohol-consumption-rising -sharply-pandemic-women/story?id=73302479.

28 Caitlin Gibson, "The End of Leaning In: How Sheryl Sandberg's Message of Empowerment Fully Unraveled," Washington Post, December 20, 2018, https://www.washingtonpost.com/life style/style/the-end-of-lean-in-how-sheryl-sandbergs-message-of -empowerment-fully-unraveled/2018/12/19/9561eb06-fe2e-11e8 -862a-b6a6f3ce8199_story.html.

29 Michelle Singletary, "Michelle Obama Is Right. We Can't Have It All," Washington Post, December 4, 2018, https://www.washing tonpost.com/business/2018/12/04/michelle-obama-is-right-we -cant-have-it-all/.

30 Gibson, "The End of Leaning In."

31 Amanda Arnold, "Oh No, a White Self-Help Guru Has Some Thoughts on Privilege," The Cut, April 7, 2021, https://www.the cut.com/2021/04/unpacking-self-help-guru-rachel-holliss-fame -and-scandals.html.

32 Samara Quintero and Jamie Long, "Toxic Positivity: The Dark Side of Positive Vibes," The Psychology Group, https://thepsychol ogygroup.com/toxic-positivity/.

33 Julia Dath, "The Pressures of Hustle Culture," Women's Opportunity Center, October 25, 2021, https://www.womensopportunity .org/woc-blog/the-pressures-of-hustle-culture.

34 Emily Paulson, phone interview with author, March 3, 2022.

35 Shaun Callaghan, Martin Lösch, Anna Pione, and Warren Teichner, "Feeling Good: The Future of the $1.5 Trillion Wellness Market," McKinsey & Company, April 8, 2021, https://www.mck insey.com/industries/consumer-packaged-goods/our-insights /feeling-good-the-future-of-the-1-5-trillion-wellness-market.

36 Rodsky, Fair Play, 34.

37 https://www.fairplaylife.com/.

38 Rodsky, Fair Play, 36.

39 Kelsey Borresen, "What Divorced Women Wish They Had Done Differently in Their Marriages," Huffington Post, last modified November 30, 2020, https://www.huffpost.com/entry/divorced -women-marriage-regrets_n_5bb4cfd5e4b0876eda9a2de0.

40 Amy Picchi, "America's Troubled Relationship with Paid Time Off for Dads," CBSNews, October 19, 2021, https://www.cbsnews.com/news/paternity-leave-pete-buttigieg-criticism-policy-united-states/.

41 Virginia Pelley, "How to Fight New-Dad Loneliness," Fatherly, April 27, 2018, https://www.fatherly.com/love-money/new-fatherhood-loneliness-solutions.

42 Alexis Barad-Cutler, "Can We Address the Real Reasons Moms Are Drinking More, Please?" Parents, June 24, 2021, https://www.parents.com/parenting/moms/can-we-address-the-real-reasons-moms-are-drinking-more-please/.

CHAPTER 4

1 Ann Dowsett Johnston, "Alcohol as Escape From Perfectionism," *The Atlantic*, October 15, 2013, http://www.theatlantic.com/health/archive/2013/10/alcohol-as-escape-from-perfectionism/280482/.

2 Yvonne, "I'm a Mom."

3 Daniel K. Hall-Flavin, "Antidepressants and Alcohol: What's the Concern?" Mayo Clinic, June 9, 2017, https://www.mayoclinic.org/diseases-conditions/depression/expert-answers/antidepressants-and-alcohol/faq-20058231#:~:text=Drinking%20can%20counteract%20the%20benefits,you%20also%20take%20another%20medication.

4 Stephanie Watson, "Alcohol and Depression," WebMD, November 15, 2020, https://www.webmd.com/depression/guide/alcohol-and-depresssion.

5 Juliana Mogielnicki, "Postpartum Depression: Who Is at Risk?" MGH Center for Women's Mental Health, June 20, 2005, https://womensmentalhealth.org/posts/postpartum-depression-who-is-at-risk/.

6 "Postpartum Anxiety," Cleveland Clinic, last modified April 12, 2022, https://my.clevelandclinic.org/health/diseases/22693-postpartum-anxiety.

7 "The Connection between Post-Partum Depression and Substance Abuse," American Addiction Centers, September 9, 2022, https://americanaddictioncenters.org/treating-depression-substance-abuse/post-partum.

8 Georgiana Wilton, D. Paul Moberg, and Michael F. Fleming, "The Effect of Brief Alcohol Intervention on Postpartum Depression," National Library of Medicine, September 15, 2009, https://www.ncbi.nlm.nih.gov/pmc/articles/PMC2743918/.

9 https://www.npr.org/sections/health-shots/2022/10/21/11291 15162/maternal-mortality-childbirth-deaths-prevention?utm_source=substack&utm_medium=email.

10 "Postpartum Depression: Causes, Symptoms, Risk Factors, and Treatment Options," American Psychological Association, 2008, https://www.apa.org/pi/women/resources/reports/postpartum-depression.

11 Julia Fraga, "Mommy Mentors Help Fight the Stigma of Postpartum Mood Disorder," NPR, September 29, 2017, https://www.npr.org/sections/health-shots/2017/09/29/554280219/mommy-mentors-help-fight-the-stigma-of-postpartum-mood-disorder.

12 Kimberly Zapata, "There's a Connection between Addiction and Mental Health," Scary Mommy, August 14, 2021, https://www.scarymommy.com/addiction-mental-health-connection.

13 Alison Brunier, "COVID-19 Pandemic Triggers 25% Increase in Prevalence of Anxiety and Depression Worldwide," World Health Organization, March 2, 2022, https://www.who.int/news/item/02-03-2022-covid-19-pandemic-triggers-25-increase-in-prevalence-of-anxiety-and-depression-worldwide.

14 Brené Brown, *Atlas of the Heart* (New York: Random House, 2021), 224.

15 Gillian Tietz, "Dr. Lembke Returns to Discuss Radical Honesty and Self-Awareness," 2022, in *Sober Powered*, produced by Gillian Tietz, podcast, 13:13, https://www.soberpowered.com/episodes/e100.

16 Barbara DeAngela, "Quotable Quotes," GoodReads, October 2 2011, https://www.goodreads.com/quotes/443878-women-need-real-moments-of-solitude-and-self-reflection-to-balance.

17 "Happiness Helps: Improve Your Mental Health with Positive Affirmations," University of Utah Health, January 12, 2021, https://healthcare.utah.edu/healthfeed/postings/2021/01/love -yourself-with-kind-words.php.

18 Ashish Sharma, Vishal Madaan, and Frederick D. Petty, "Exercise for Mental Health," *Primary Care Companion to the Journal of Clinical Psychiatry* 8, no. 2 (2006): 106. https://doi.org/10.4088/pcc.v08n0208a.

CHAPTER 5

1 Zoe Williams, "Anne Hathaway Is Giving Up Booze for 18 Years To Be a Better Mother," *The Guardian*, January 25, 2019, https:// www.theguardian.com/lifeandstyle/shortcuts/2019/jan/25/anne -hathaway-giving-up-booze-better-mother-cant-drink-to-that.

2 Name changed for privacy.

3 Barry, "Dear Mothers."

4 Margaret Heffernan, on Quotes.pub, https://quotes.pub/q/we -know-intellectually-that-confronting-an-issue-is-the-only-610518.

5 Rachel Tepper Paley, "Meme Girls: The Wine Mom Phenomenon Speaks Volumes," Wine Enthusiast, March 23, 2021, https://www .winemag.com/2021/03/23/wine-mom-phenomenon-memes/.

6 Vena Moore, "Wine Mom Culture Excludes Black Mothers," Medium, February 28, 2022, https://medium.com/fourth-wave /wine-mom-culture-excludes-black-mothers-6145dee74324.

7 Tepper Paley, "Meme Girls."

8 Dowsett Johnston, *Drink*, 66.

9 Aneri Pattani, "Women Now Drink as Much as Men—And Are Prone to Sickness Sooner," KHN, June 9, 2021, https://khn.org /news/article/women-now-drink-as-much-as-men-and-are-prone -to-sickness-sooner/.

10 Samantha O'Brien, "'It's Not Alcoholism Until You Graduate': Insight into College Binge Drinking Culture," Millennium Counseling Center, August 30, 2018, https://millenniumhope.com/not -alcoholism-until-you-graduate-college-binge-drinking-culture/.

11 "Alcohol and Drug Information," Allan Hancock College Health Services, last modified October 10, 2022, https://www.hancock college.edu/studenthealth/alcohol.php?locale=en#:~:text=Alco hol%20Abuse%20and%20Dependence%3A%2031,et%20al .%2C%202002.

12 Carol Galbicsek, "College Alcoholism," Alcohol Rehab Guide, September 21, 2022, https://www.alcoholrehabguide.org/resources /college-alcohol-abuse/.

13 "Campus Sexual Violence: Statistics," Rainn, 2022, https://www .rainn.org/statistics/campus-sexual-violence.

14 "Is Binge Drinking in College Worth a Lifetime of Damage and Health Issues?" University of Nevada, Reno, https://onlinede grees.unr.edu/blog/binge-drinking-in-college/.

15 "College Drinking," National Institute on Alcohol Abuse and Alcoholism, last modified June 2022, https://www.niaaa.nih.gov /publications/brochures-and-fact-sheets/college-drinking#:~: text=Factors%20Affecting%20Student%20Drinking&text=In %20fact%2C%20college%20students%20have,alcohol%20 than%20their%20noncollege%20peers.

16 "College Drinking."

17 Katie Feuerstein, "Toxic Drinking Culture Haunts the American 'Normal,'" Access Health, March 27, 2022, https://accesshealth news.net/toxic-drinking-culture-haunts-the-american-normal/.

18 Ashley Fetters, "The Many Faces of the 'Wine Mom,'" The Atlan-tic, May 23, 2020, https://www.theatlantic.com/family/archive /2020/05/wine-moms-explained/612001/.

19 Whitaker, *Quit Like a Woman*, 59.

20 Jessica Lahey, *The Addiction Inoculation* (New York: HarperCollins, 2021), 33.

21 Lahey, *The Addiction Inoculation*, 79.

22 Lahey, *The Addiction Inoculation*, 163.

23 "Sundar Pichai Is Ending Google's Once Famous Partying Culture by Limiting Drinking at Work and Threatening 'More Onerous Actions,'" BusinessInsider, November 8, 2018, https://www.busi

nessinsider.com/google-limits-alcohol-at-work-in-sexual-harass
ment-crack-down-2018-11.
24 Flip Prior, "Navigating Drinking Culture in the Workplace When
You're Sober," ABC Everyday, last modified October 29, 2019,
https://www.abc.net.au/everyday/navigating-drinking-culture
-in-the-workplace-when-youre-sober/11589836.
25 "Drinking Alcohol," Breastcancer.org, last modified August 29,
2022, https://www.breastcancer.org/risk/factors/alcohol.

CHAPTER 6

1 Elise Hu and Audrey Nguyen, "Too Much Pleasure Can Lead to
Addiction. How To Break the Cycle and Find Balance," NPR, April
4, 2022, https://www.npr.org/2022/03/31/1090009509/addiction
-how-to-break-the-cycle-and-find-balance.
2 Sandee LaMotte and Jen Christensen, "No Amount of Alcohol Is
Good for the Heart, New Report Says, but Critics Disagree on Science," CNN Health, last modified January 20, 2022, https://www
.cnn.com/2022/01/20/health/no-alcohol-good-for-heart-well
ness/index.html#:~:text=Drinking%20alcohol%20increases
%20the%20risk,of%20healthy%20life%2C%20it%20says.
3 Watson, "Alcohol and Depression."
4 Ruby Warrington, Sober Curious (New York: HarperOne, 2019),
http://www.rubywarrington.com/books/sober-curious/.
5 "Sober Curious? A Brief History, Benefits, and How to Start,"
Surely, January 29, 2021, https://www.hisurely.com/a/blog/sober
-curious-a-brief-history-benefits-and-how-to-start#table-of-con
tents-1.
6 Catherine Gray, *The Unexpected Joy of Being Sober* (London: Octopus,
2017), 45.
7 Jordan Valinsky, "Dry January Was More Popular Than Ever.
That's Good News for the Alcohol Industry," CNN Business, February 16, 2022, https://www.cnn.com/2022/02/16/business/dry
-january-participation-2022/index.html.

CHAPTER 7

1 American Addiction Centers Resource, "Holiday Binge Drinking," October 25, 2022, https://alcohol.org/statistics-information/holiday-binge-drinking/.

2 "Understanding Alcohol Use Disorder," National Institute on Alcohol Abuse and Alcoholism, last modified April 2021, https://www.niaaa.nih.gov/publications/brochures-and-fact-sheets/understanding-alcohol-use-disorder.

3 Kari Schwear, "What Is Gray Area Drinking?" Graytonic (blog), https://www.graytonic.com/what-is-gray-area-drinking/.

4 "Drinking Levels Defined," National Institute on Alcohol Abuse and Alcoholism, 2020, https://www.niaaa.nih.gov/alcohol-health/overview-alcohol-consumption/moderate-binge-drinking.

5 Dowsett Johnston, *Drink*, 59.

6 Anna Lembke, *Dopamine Nation* (New York: Dutton, 2021), 72–88.

7 Lembke, *Dopamine Nation*, 72–88.

8 Victor Yalom and Rebecca Aponte, "Alan Marlatt on Harm Reduction Therapy," Psychotherapy.net, 2011, https://www.psychotherapy.net/interview/marlatt-harm-reduction.

9 "Mom Perfectly Explains 'Daddy Privilege' in Viral TikTok: 'He's Not a Hero, He's a Father,'" In the Know, November 29, 2021, https://www.intheknow.com/post/mom-explains-daddy-privilege/.

10 Celeste Yvonne (@theultimatemomchallenge), "Interview with Annie Grace from This Naked Mind," Instagram video, September 18, 2019, https://www.instagram.com/tv/B2kOBdlHigm/?igshid=YmMyMTA2M2Y=.

11 Amanda White, interview with the author, June 9, 2022.

12 Gray, *The Unexpected Joy*, 98.

13 "What Is Exposure Therapy?" American Psychological Association, July 2017, https://www.apa.org/ptsd-guideline/patients-and-families/exposure-therapy.

14 Manny Chinnis, "How Long Does PAWS Last? Post-Acute Withdrawal Symptoms," Atlanta Recovery Place, June 22, 2021, https://atlantarecoveryplace.com/how-long-does-paws-last/.

CHAPTER 8

1 Laura McKowen, *We Are the Luckiest* (Novato, CA: New World Library), 182.
2 McKowen, *We Are the Luckiest*, 182.
3 Amy Weatherly and Jess Johnston, *I'll Be There (But I'll Be Wearing Sweatpants)* (Nashville, TN: Thomas Nelson, 2022), 14.
4 Perri Ormont Blumberg, "How To Make (and Keep) Friends as an Adult, According to Experts," Today, August 12, 2022, https://www.today.com/health/how-long-does-it-take-make-friend-friendship-advice-t126538.
5 Michael Ascher, "The Opposite of Addiction Is Not Sobriety—It Is Human Connection," aschermd.com, 1981, https://aschermd.com/the-opposite-of-addiction-is-not-sobriety-it-is-human-connection/#:~:text=In%20an%20increasingly%20popular%20TED,sobriety%2C%20it%20is%20human%20connection.
6 Mindy Manwarren Generes, ed., "Psychotherapy Guide: Group Therapy vs. Individual Therapy," American Addiction Centers, September 12, 2022, https://americanaddictioncenters.org/therapy-treatment/group-individual.
7 Glennon Doyle, "Friendship: What Is It and Why Do We Need It Now More Than Ever?" January 25, 2022, in *We Can Do Hard Things*, podcast, 17:28, https://podcasts.apple.com/us/podcast/we-can-do-hard-things-with-glennon-doyle/id1564530722?i=1000548902280.
8 Ann Lamott, "Kick Guilt to the Gutter for Moms in Recovery—3 Proven Tips That Work!" Sober Moms Guide, October 9, 2019, https://www.sobermomsguide.com/blog?tag=guilt.
9 Weatherly and Johnston, *I'll Be There*, 26.

CHAPTER 9

1 Gray, *The Unexpected Joy*, 14.
2 Veronica Valli webinar with Sober Mom Squad on February 11, 2021.

3 Veronica Valli, *Soberful* (Boulder, CO: Sounds True, 2022), 237.

4 TheChosenOnez, "Trying To Hurt Me," ifunny.co, February 5, 2021, https://ifunny.co/picture/trying-to-hurt-me-by-bringing-up -my-past-is-yIB23D0M8.